T0268036

'This book is written by Khwaja Ahmad Abbas, who gave me my first film, *Saat Hindustani*. I called him Mamujaan. The book is a deep, incisive look at the gold-and-silver world of cinema. The sheen wears off but the spirit lives on. Khwaja Ahmed Abbas Trust keeps Abbas Saheb's unrelenting spirit effervescent. The book features illustrious, legendary men and women who rode the crest—barring one, of course, a certain Amitabh Bachchan—and men and women who were subalterns of cinema (and with whom Abbas Saheb had personal, vivid interactions). The original Urdu is now before the world in its English translation.

As the poet said:

मेरी तस्वीर के ये नक़्श ज़रा गौर से देख;
इस में इक दौर की तस्वीर नज़र आएगी।

—**Amitabh Bachchan**

'This book shines a light on idols of gold and silver, the film persona featured in this first English translation from the original. K.A. Abbas wrote seventy-four books in his seventy-three-year life span. Filmi *sitarey* move through the pages along with the top directors, poets, technicians—from the *qalam* of a man who referred to himself as *Azad Qalam*, one who was in the midst of it all yet could detach himself and watch the filmi kaleidoscope unfold. It is an interesting read'—**Shabana Azmi**

'Raj Kapoor and Khwaja Ahmad Abbas shared a very special relationship. As friends and frequent collaborators, they understood one another and shared the same ethos. This insightful book sheds light on facets of the film industry as seen through the eyes of Abbas. A must-read for film lovers' —**Randhir Kapoor**

'In *Sone Chandi ke Buth*, screenwriter and journalist Khwaja Ahmad Abbas takes us behind the scenes to reveal lesser-known aspects of the film industry. Like his films, his writing also reflects his humanistic ideals, brought alive in many of Raj Kapoor Sahab's films. It is wonderful to see these translations brought forward through this collection'—**Rahul Rawail**

SONE CHANDI
KE BUTH

'As a writer, film critic, screenwriter and film-maker, and one committed to the values of social justice, and driven by a diagnostic and curative vision of the goals of art, K.A. Abbas represents a crucial figure of the Indian modern who believed that critics and artists had a responsibility towards society. Bringing together translations from the original Urdu published pieces of his writings on cinema along with his articles in the *Bombay Chronicle*, *Sone Chandi ke Buth*, edited by Syeda Hameed and Sukhpreet Kahlon, is a very welcome edition that foregrounds the commitment and values of art and journalism at a very crucial moment in our time'—**Prof. Ira Bhaskar**

SONE CHANDI KE BUTH

Writings on Cinema

KHWAJA AHMAD ABBAS

Edited and translated by
SYEDA HAMEED *and*
SUKHPREET KAHLON

VINTAGE
An imprint of Penguin Random House

VINTAGE

USA | Canada | UK | Ireland | Australia
New Zealand | India | South Africa | China

Vintage is part of the Penguin Random House group of companies
whose addresses can be found at global.penguinrandomhouse.com

Published by Penguin Random House India Pvt. Ltd
4th Floor, Capital Tower 1, MG Road,
Gurugram 122 002, Haryana, India

First published in Vintage by Penguin Random House India 2022

Copyright © K.A. Abbas 2022
Translation copyright © Syeda Hameed and Sukhpreet Kahlon 2022

ISBN 9780670095933

Typeset in RequiemText by Manipal Technologies Limited, Manipal
Printed at Thomson Press India Ltd, New Delhi

www.penguin.co.in

Contents

KAHAANIYAAN

ARTICLES

BOMBAY CHRONICLE ARTICLES

Preface

A book lies before us as we write these lines: *Sone Chandi ke Buth* by Khwaja Ahmad Abbas. It is tattered, each page is loose, the cover is a dirty purple, torn and worn. While we worked on its translation we dared not hand it to a book binder. Its condition and the condition of most of Abbas's works is best described by Allama Iqbal in this couplet:

Uday kuchh waraq bulbul ne kuchh laaley ne kuchh gul ne
Chaman mein har taraf bikhri hui hai daastaan meri

Some pages were blown away
By the poppy, the nightingale, the rose
My story lies scattered all over the garden.

The man wrote seventy-four books in seventy-three years; so few have survived! This includes 3000 pieces of journalese, the longest running weekly column, forty-six years nonstop in *Blitz*, forty films (thirteen under the Naya Sansar banner), and mastery over three languages—Urdu, Hindi and English. Whatever little survives, lies with the Khwaja Ahmed Abbas Memorial Trust from where this literary gem was excavated.

Sone Chandi ke Buth is Abbas's last word on the filmi *duniya*. He passed away one year after the book was published. The boy from Panipat, land of Sufis, land of battles, went from the Qasba taking his sensibilities to India's phantasmagoria. *Bambai Raat ki Bahon Mein* is the title of one of his thirteen films which flopped at the box office but is one of the most incisive films about the underbelly of glamour. He was the child of a deeply religious, liberal, reformist family, best known through its three great ancestors, Maulana Altaf Husain Hali, Khwaja Ghulamus Saqlain and Khwaja Ghulamus Sibtain. The first was India's first feminist poet, the second a member of the legislative council but the more important one whose travelogues are world classics. The third was a reformist and educationist, pristine and principled. None could have dreamt that their beloved child would wander in the gullies of the forbidden city. Abbas shattered their dreams. He became neither a lawyer nor a teacher, he only wrote, wrote and wrote. As his beloved friend Krishan Chander wrote in his preface to Abbas's short-story collection *Paoon Mein Phool*, 'Abbas's pen rides on rubber tyres. It has the speed of wind and the velocity of sound.' He wrote in trains, buses and airplanes; after meeting Yuri Gagarin in Moscow, he wrote half his book *Till we Reach the Stars* on the return Aeroflot flight to Bombay.

This book is an insider's view of the 'Sitaron ki Duniya'. He writes about the thespians, the *chamaktey sitarey*, the technicians, the extras, the light-coolies, the dreamers, the losers, all of them with the same delicate touch. There is no hierarchy in his mind; Chavli 'chamarin' in *Char Dil Char Rahein* rides the crest as does

Stella the ayah in the same film. Salma the rickshaw puller's daughter in *Aasmaan Mahal* is touched with the same brush as her lover, the Nawabzada. Two lines of a song from the film exemplify his view on class:

Sone chandi ki tamanna hai na resham ki talaash
Khaak hai khaak ye daulat ka sunehra aakaash
Teri aankhon hee main aabaad hai jannat meri.

No desire for gold or silver, no quest for silk
Canopy of dust, this gold-crafted sky
My paradise dwells in your very eyes.

The original book is divided into three parts: Mazameen, Funn Aur Funkaar and Kahaaniyaan. The first two are based on Abbas's lived life in his modest flat in Juhu. There are the giants of Indian cinema, women and men who strode the stage of life which doubled as film! There is the changing world of cinema—realism pitted against pure entertainment; hunger, which compels a mother to dope her baby to stay silent during a film shot. The story section is Abbas drawing a thin curtain over well-loved film icons to tell their story with new names. Some of us, who have lived in that era, can recognize the faces and incidents. But it hardly matters because the stories stand on their own.

The man who introduced to Bombay cinema its brightest stars, whether Amitabh Bachchan, Smita Patil, Shabana Azmi, Mithun Chakraborty and some lesser knowns but also of stellar quality like Jalal Agha, Persis Khambata, Dilip Raj and Surekha, has given his candid assessment of this world in this museum of statues. The story of Prophet Abraham's father, Aazar the sculptor, is well known. While he made statues, his son was the first prophet who taught humanity the concept of monotheism. Abbas's story is the reverse. His ancestors were monotheists but he was the maker of idols of gold and silver. Allama Iqbal sums up the philosophy of *Sone Chandi ke Buth*:

Tere bhi sanam khaney mere bhi sanam khaney
Dono ke sanam khaaki dono ke sanam faani

Thou hast thy pantheon and I have mine O Lord
Both are idols of dust . . . both are idols that die

Introduction

K.A. Abbas was a man in a hurry.

Mujhe kuchh kehna hai—I have to say something. Short stories, articles, novels, dramas, films—all these forms of expression seemed to burst out of the man called 'human dynamo' by his closest friends. Today, multiple screens flash past our bedazzled eyes. In those hoardings, the film world is ubiquitous; whether it is *RRR* (Rajmouli Ram Charan Rama Rao, 2022) or *Bachchan Pandey* (2022) or *Gangubai Kathiawadi* (2022). Or the gigantic hoardings of film stars like Akshay Kumar and Shahrukh Khan in blue jeans advertising Kajaria tiles and Omany tiles respectively. Blue is true!

But Abbas lived in a different age; it was a different sensibility in which he worked.

He had many friends, of whom three names readily come to mind: Krishan Chander, Ali Sardar Jafri and Rajinder Singh Bedi. Of them, only Jafri Sahib was alive when Abbas lay dying, so he assigned him a duty at his funeral. This was recorded in the will he published on 13 June 1987 in his column 'Last Page' of *Blitz*: The Last Will and Testament of Khwaja Ahmad Abbas.

No one but Abbas could have written such a will. Instead of an official stamp, the stamp was Abbas! Abbas! Abbas! He wrote that his funeral procession should be headed by a Maharashtrian Lazim band. And that his bier should be carried on a lorry driven along the sea front in Juhu, which he loved. He had nothing to leave for posterity but his writings, 'over 70 books', through which anyone could meet him at any time.

'I am an agnostic, meaning I don't know enough about religion. I believe in One God but all religions believe in One Divinity.'

He wrote each detail of his memorial meeting. It should be a 'celebration', he said, with five-minute speeches by friends, whom he named, from all religions.

One word was for the publisher of *Blitz*: He could retain the name of his column 'Last Page' and 'Azad Qalam' and 'entrust it to one like P. Sainath who will carry the Abbas tradition'. In the end was just 'LOVE', showered over all who cared for a man called KAA.

*   *   *

Abbas came from a family of poets and writers. Panipat, where his entire family lived for 800 years before Partition, was a land of Sufis and scholars. He recorded in his autobiography, *I Am Not an Island*,[1] that his earliest ancestors were Sufi scholars and teachers who came to Panipat from Herat (then part of greater Iran) in the thirteenth century during the rule of Sultan Ghiyasuddin Balban. They settled there due to the largesse of

---

[1] *I Am Not an Island: An Experiment in Autobiography*, Vikas Publishing House, 1977

a ruler who honoured scholars like Khwaja Malik Ali, Khwaja Ahmad Abbas's earliest known ancestor. Several years post Partition, Abbas visited his now occupied ancestral home in search of his birth certificate. He knew it had been carefully stored but it was gone from the ravaged *tehkhana* of his home. Since then, he always called himself 'a man without a birth certificate'.

In his Introduction to *Sone Chandi ke Buth*, Abbas did not use the two Urdu words for Preface or Introduction, *Tamheed* or *Pesh Lafz*. He simply wrote '*Mujhe kuchh kehna hai*'. The date below this piece was 4 February 1986; it was his last major work. Sixteen months later he was dead. His last film *Ek Aadmi* (1988) was released posthumously, but this book he saw in print. It was his last comment on the gold and silver idols towering over the Bombay skyline.

The sense he had of life's end was perhaps why he wrote that his article 'Film Mein Jeena, Film Mein Marna' (Living for Films, Dying for Films) was the 'key' piece in his book. 'From all parts of the country "they" arrive in this bustling world of make belief, fantasy, glamour, above all endless wealth.' And once they tasted this heady potion, they rarely returned home. He mentioned a particular youth from Jind in Haryana, who would leave his pillow and chador in a paan wallah's stall and spend his day trudging from studio to studio, searching for the lucky break.

In the articles included in this book, we hear the voice of Abbas the teacher, Abbas the child of Sufi masters, admonishing these wannabes: 'Have you ever written a story? Have you ever acted in a play? Have you ever sung in a mehfil? No? Then go back. Try all this and more. Then return and with confidence find your niche in the filmi *duniya*; the producers will run after you. Look in the mirror. Growing sideburns like your favourite movie star and mimicking his gait is not enough.' Perhaps he was thinking of a song from the film *Albela* (1951) when he wrote these lines. It was sung on the screen by the matchless comedian Bhagwan:

Badi akad se beta nikla ghar se actor hone
Wah ri qismat, qismat mein likhe tthe kapde dhone

Swaggering the son left home for becoming an actor
Alas the fate! His destiny was to wash dirty clothes.

When it came to Abbas's relationship with the tallest icon of Bollywood, there hung a story. Amitabh Bachchan had come to his door at the behest of his assistant director, Tinnu Anand. Abbas looked him up and down, but first and foremost saw him as the son of his old friend Harivansh Rai. Before considering him for the role of Anwar Ali in his film *Saat Hindustani* (about the liberation of Goa), he sought the permission of his friend. Only when this arrived via a telegram did he launch the man who was destined to rule Bollywood for four decades or more.

In his autobiography, Abbas looked back on his first foray into films. This came during his initial days at *Bombay Chronicle,* edited by the legendary Abdulla Barelvi. 'The *Bombay Chronicle* office near Flora Fountain was a rickety two-storey beehive, a building mostly made of wood which had a rotary machine on the ground floor. When started, it shook the whole building. It was an earthquake which rocked the wooden structure several times a day. I was surprised how they managed to write in such an unstable atmosphere, but within two weeks I was used, attuned would be more appropriate, to it.'

Finding it hard to survive on the paltry salary of a journalist, Abbas decided to write film publicity for some of the studios as he found the quality of their writing mediocre. 'They sent out copies of the same badly written blurb, prepared by some illiterate hack,' he wrote. So, he met Himanshu Rai, who had started Bombay Talkies with his wife Devika Rani. Rai offered Abbas Rs 75 a month for writing publicity blurbs, a princely sum for a journalist!

I didn't understand him at first, when I did I felt dizzy. Fifty rupees a month for twenty-six days of back-breaking office work, and seventy-five rupees for just four days that would be a kind of Sunday picnic! I would scribble the stuff in the train, type it in the studio, and be free before lunch. Lunch which I would get free in the studio cafeteria.

I accepted the terms, and it was the beginning of a long friendship with Himanshu Rai, and Devika Rani, with various other members of their staff including Sasadhar Mukerji and a shy and reticent Ashok Kumar (I remember the day when he was taken out of the laboratory where, being a science graduate, he was working as an assistant, and asked to do the make-up for Jeevan Naiya). His first shot was jumping into a room through a window, and I got a brainwave. 'Ashok Kumar Crashes into Stardom', was the obvious headline of a blurb that I wrote for the occasion. Himanshu Rai, once actor, then producer, had an obsession with respectability and education. 'Bring me a graduate from a good family and I will make him into an actor.' Ashok Kumar is certainly an advertisement of his methods.

Film publicity was Abbas's own 'crashing' into the world
of films, a world that would mesmerize and immerse him
for the rest of his life. While at *Bombay Chronicle*, he even got
the opportunity to work as a film critic. In his profile of V.
Shantaram in this book, he described how that happened. The
staffer of the review page was away so Barelvi Sahib asked
Abbas to pitch in. Right at the start he rocked the sedate boat
of film reviews. In his autobiography, he notes,

> My editor gave me complete liberty to be as critical as I
> wanted to be, but he advised me that when I wanted to be
> very critical I should use as abstruse words as possible. For
> instance, he said when you want to say a film is lousy, say
> it is inconsequential; when you want to say that a script is
> rotten, say it is putrid. 'The producers don't know much
> English—so they won't be offended, while the intelligent
> readers will get your message.'

He then went on to write of his travails as a film critic, a role which
was ultimately taken away from him when he was 'kicked upstairs',
meaning he was given a senior slot to get him out of the way!

> Mr Barelvi was woefully misinformed about the
> educational level of film producers. Evidently quite a few
> of them or at least someone in their entourage of hangers
> on, currently called *chamchas,* were able to understand
> that here was a critic who was lambasting most of their
> pictures. They made written complaints, then some of
> them came over and charged me with being prejudiced
> against Indian films generally. They hinted at withdrawal
> of all film advertising from the *Chronicle*.

My editor sent me their written complaints, and later called me over for a personal chat. Before the matter went over to the proprietor, he advised me to ignore the pictures that were very bad, and to dismiss the others in a paragraph or two. 'But if you really come across an unusual, interesting and distinguished picture, go all out to praise it—so the very length of the review will make it obvious to the readers that this is the one picture that you recommended.

Bombay Chronicle later confirmed him as a film critic, and for three years, he saw some 300 Indian and foreign films a year. He admitted to watching Shantaram's *Aadmi* (1939) twenty-five times and *Duniya Na Mane* (1937) eighteen times.

Shantaram was Abbas the film critic's entry into Marathi films. He was ecstatic about three of his films: *Duniya Na Mane*, *Aadmi* and *Padosi* (1941). He wrote that he learnt his most precious lessons from this doyen of films. Abbas considered his later hit films such as *Jhanak Jhanak Payal Baje* (1955) technically perfect, but averred that they were much lesser than his initial classics. On Shantaram's request, he wrote the story and screenplay of *Dr Kotnis Ki Amar Kahani* (1946) in which the doyen played the title role. Abbas had high praise for his acting talent in every role he essayed, whether as Dr Kotnis or as the jailor in *Do Ankhen Barah Haath* (1957).

The last sentence in this article is typical Abbas: candid and uncompromising even of the closest and the best. The sentence also explains why Abbas with his meagre earnings would survive while many box office moguls would be forgotten. First, he called Shantaram 'sadabahar' at eighty plus. He wrote that while addressing a public function, in the presence of

Shantaram, he spoke a line which said it all. 'It is essential that film students and film practitioners should study classics like *Aadmi* and *Duniya Na Mane*,' he said, adding, 'Shantaram himself should be part of that study circle.'

* * *

Sone Chandi ke Buth was Abbas's swan song. As he said in his short foreword to the book, '*Iss thaili main sab kuchh hai pyare*' (This bag of tricks has it all). The three sections were named Mazameen, Funn Aur Funkaar, Kahaaniyaan, all about the glitz and glamour, tryst and tragedy of the filmi *duniya*. In some pieces the characters strode the stage of life in full form, in some there was a fine veil over the real-life subject, a veil which revealed more than it concealed. It was Abbas's truth as he saw it, and he cared little about ruffling feathers of the mighty and powerful. He lived by the creed of his great-grandfather, Maulana Altaf Husain Hali, India's first feminist and finest reformist poet. Hali's description of Mirza Ghalib was a perfect fit for his own grandson Abbas:

Khaaksaaron se khaaksaari thhee
Sar bulandon se inkisaar na ttha

Humility with the humble
No ingratiation with the imperious

* * *

In 1980, in an interview for *Indian Literary Review*, his young friend and protege Suresh Kohli asked Abbas Sahib about the film he was making. Reading his answer reminds one of Amitabh Bachchan describing him as the 'Man Who Saw Tomorrow'.

'I am making the *Naxalites*, a very dangerous film. I feel scared of being shot at from both sides. Though I think it is neither a glorification nor denigration of Naxalites. I only hope that the film is not misunderstood as my story *Sardarji* was.'

He was then asked what gave him the idea to make a film on Naxalites? 'I was excited by these people who are willing to do or die, to kill or die. And I said to myself that here is a great drama. A great human drama was waiting to be told in which people can be so motivated and so dedicated to an ideal that they will kill or be killed. I thought it could be worth analysing. And also, because I had a theory of my own which might be purely subjective, that this thing is rooted in Bengal famine of 1943; that the first Naxalite was a baby at that time and in their subconsciousness lurked the bitterness of the Calcutta pavements. That is what I have tried to show in this film.'

Krishan Chander, one of Abbas' closest friends, wrote in the foreword, which defines Abbas, to his short story *Paoon Mein Phool*:

As Inquilab strengthens in India Abbas writings will become increasingly luminous. But . . . if there is counter revolution and fascism becomes order of the day the first to be thrown in fire will be Abbas's writings.[2]

2   Krishan Chander's Preface to K.A. Abbas' short story collection *Paoon Mein Phool* in Kulliyaat K.A. Abbas (8 Volumes) edited by Iritiza Karim, National Council for Promotion of Urdu Language, 2017

Krishan Chander was referring to the 1933 book burnings in Germany known as Bibliocaust. Students burnt 25,000 books, shouting slogans in support of the regime. Heinrich Heine, a nineteenth-century German writer, had prophesied, 'Where one burns books one will soon burn people.'

So, dear reader! Judge Abbas for yourselves as the one who sculpted this '*adhbudh*' *Sone Chandi ke Buth* for your reading pleasure.

Syeda Hameed and Sukhpreet Kahlon
Delhi, 2022

I Have Something to Say

Film Industry

For the last forty-five years, I have been in conflict with the word 'industry' being used for films. At the Motion Pictures Congress, I announced my opposition to it.

I said, don't consider films an industry in the manner of cloth mills or steel factories. Film is both art and science; it is the collective endeavour of many. It needs many technical inputs—photography, sound and make-up which turns age to youth and vice versa. Calling it an industry is an insult to all aspects of this art. Camera manufacture and manufacture of sound equipment can be called an industry. Film is a creative art, born in the mind of the artist and produced by a collective. In terms of hierarchy, first comes the director, then the story writer and then the screenplay or dialogue writer. Next in line is the camera expert and then the editor—the latter is a very special team member. Then the actors, actresses and sound recordists and, finally, the music director. The last is India's favourite team member. Seven elements combine to produce the eighth art.

It is only when we consider film an art that we experience its social impact. Film is no longer the 'moving picture' we used to watch as children. People like Debaki Bose, P.C. Barua, Shantaram, Mehboob Khan, Satyajit Ray and other directors made us understand the power of this medium through which a collective influences a huge audience, makes them laugh, cry and think—this is the creative miracle of the film media.

Our misfortune is that by calling film an industry we have trivialized its creativity. We are so preoccupied with its financial ups and downs that it no longer remains an artistic endeavour; it becomes a creature of the black market. I don't know whether this is our own misfortune or the misfortune of our art. I think of actors—Sanjiv Kumar, perhaps because he is not with us any more or before him others such as Sehgal, Pankaj Mullick, Vinayak and Guru Dutt. They were all fine actors but not idols of silver and gold. But today there are Raj Kapoor, Dilip Kumar and Amitabh Bachchan. In the temple of the film universe, they are weighed in gold, silver and crores.

In this book, *Sone Chandi ke Buth* (Idols of Silver and Gold), I have drawn a few of their sketches. I have also written a few stories in which I have drawn a veil over the faces of these gold and silver idols. There are some articles as well, key among which is 'Living for Films, Dying for Films'.

The film world is mapped in my stories. Successful artists, failed artists, silver-gold idols, old hands and new faces . . . you will see them all. In this magic box, you will find them all. Film

is an art, friends. All endeavours to turn it into a gold standard
or silver measure are bound to fail.

K.A. Abbas
4 February 1986

FUNN AUR FUNKAAR

The first section of *Sone Chandi ke Buth* is a set of profiles written by Khwaja Ahmad Abbas on film personalities. From actors to writers and filmmakers, these sketches, written in his frank, inimitable style, enable us to see these artists through Abbas's eyes.

Making a distinction between actors of yesteryears and those whom he sees around him, he reflects on the immense stardom of film personalities and wonders at their value, which is measured in gold, silver and crores of rupees. Through these sketches, we learn about the people behind the silver screen, their career trajectories and impact as artists.

Abbas's sheer love for Raj Kapoor, his unabashed admiration for Meena Kumari, his first meeting with the superstar of Hindi cinema Amitabh Bachchan, his displeasure at Dilip Kumar's career choices, deep respect for Balraj Sahni, camaraderie with Sahir Ludhianvi and other such moments offer insights into Abbas as well as the people whom he writes about. In these sketches, what stands out the most is perhaps Abbas's candidness in his observations, a rare quality in the film journalism of today.

V. Shantaram: The Evergreen Film-maker

I came to Bombay in 1936. At the time, like many people, I used to think that artistic films made in India were in some way or the other related to Bengali cinema. I was under the impression that only action films and a few select social films were made in Bombay, and those too pertained to an archaic style that concentrated on issues within the family and ended on a happy note. In those days, Debaki Bose (*Rajrani Meera*, 1933, *Seeta*, 1934), Nitin Bose (*Chandidas*, 1934, *President*, 1937) and P.C. Barua (*Devdas*, 1935, *Manzil*, 1936) were filmmakers of renown.

In 1937, a bilingual film was released. Made in Pune, it was called *Kunku* in Marathi and *Duniya Na Mane* in Hindi. At the time, Kanhaiya Lal Vakil was the film critic for the *Bombay Chronicle* (he was also the art critic for the same newspaper). He received an invitation for the premiere of *Duniya Na Mane* but had to attend an art exhibition that same evening. He handed me the invitation and asked me to write about the film. If it hadn't been for this, I would have perhaps not watched the film

at all. Certain bare truths were poetically presented in the film.
The camera angles and fusing of different shots were a real treat
for the eyes. The other aspect that stood out, apart from these,
was the character of the protagonist, Shanta Apte, who refuses
to get married against her wishes or make any compromise in
the matter. Watching this film was almost a revelation for me.
The film had rejected the intellectually bereft commercial films
of Bombay and escaped the beautiful but lifeless romance of
the Calcutta school, embracing a new direction.

The exceptional wizardry of *Duniya Na Mane* introduced
me to the creative personage of V. Shantaram. I wrote a long
article—but worth reading, in my opinion—about the film.
This was one of my best pieces as a film critic. It did not escape
the sharp eyes of my editor, and within a year, after the sad
demise of Kanhaiya Lal, I was made the film critic. I was to
continue with my responsibility as a sub-editor alongside.

A year later, the film *Aadmi (1939)* was released. In my
opinion, Shantaram should be remembered for this remarkable
film. Not only was the realistic portrayal of the characters
and their habitat exceptional, but the use of satire and the
technically adept use of editing, sound and montage made the
film an exemplar of artistic standards.

Apart from its masterful presentation, the film had a
philosophical theme and conveyed a social message. It was
also obvious that the sensational character of the rebellious
woman was not a mere coincidence. In *Aadmi*, the character
of the courtesan (which Shanta Hublikar has made immortal)
is socially pertinent and displays psychological depth. Most
significantly, the climax is a realistic one. Two years prior to
this film, *Devdas* left a mark and deeply influenced the youth.
The film presented a gilded version of the sorrows and woes of

life, making it far removed from the truth. *Aadmi* rejects such a sentiment entirely.

I remember I dedicated all seven columns of my film review page to this unique film, setting a record in the history of film criticism, in India and perhaps in the world. Every reader was extremely surprised and took notice of the film. I remember I received several letters from people who usually look down upon Indian films but on reading this long column were compelled to watch *Aadmi*.

Shantaram (whom I had not yet met) called me himself and invited me to watch the film again. This invitation was extended to me because at the end of my column I had written that to completely understand the social relevance and artistic importance of the film, I would have to watch it repeatedly.

My subsequent meetings with Shantaram took me from Bombay to Prabhat Studios in Pune. Our meetings continued even after he separated from the partners of Prabhat Studios and moved to Bombay. However, whenever I met him, it was this film that would somehow become the topic of discussion. Sometimes, we would argue on the art and technique of cinema and the interrelationship between the two; at other times we would contemplate the social relevance of this powerful medium from a critical perspective. As time passed, I started to become a specialist in Shantaram's films.

I gained this expertise with a lot of hard work. I watched *Duniya Na Mane* eighteen times and *Aadmi* twenty-four times! Relying on my memory, I even wrote the screenplay of *Aadmi* (I wrote the screenplay of Nitin Bose's *President* in this manner as well). Once Shantaram and I had a difference of opinion on a small issue related to *Aadmi*. To settle matters, we watched the film again and only then was he convinced that I was indeed correct.

I wrote the screenplays of *Duniya Na Mane, Aadmi, President, Dharti Mata* (1938), *The Story of Louis Pasteur* (1936) and a few other films after watching them repeatedly. It has been my endeavour from the very beginning to understand films and collect information on them. This endeavour has served as a foundation and instilled confidence in me to direct films. I learnt the finer points of cinema from Shantaram and his films. The principles seen in his early films and their social relevance influenced his creativity. This is especially evident in his film *Padosi* (1941). The film has a straightforward story that examines the resentment that develops between two friends and deals with the theme of national integration. It is among the best films made in the country.

The razzmatazz and escapism seen in the unnecessary romantic part of the film appears for the first time in a Shantaram film, thereby compromising what was otherwise an eminent piece of work.

Thereafter, Shantaram started to get increasingly involved in the splendour and production value of his films and focused less on content and realism.

Shantaram's later films are not as satisfactory in terms of artistic value. Despite this, they are technically brilliant and the talent of the actors, selected and trained by him, bear testimony to his genius. I have learnt so much from him. In fact, there are very few who have not gained something or the other from him.

During his long and unforgettable career in Bombay, he made two films which must be especially mentioned. One is *Dr Kotnis Ki Amar Kahani* (1946), which was based on my screenplay (I wrote it along with my friend V.P. Sathe). In this, the true story of the courage and dedication, daring and martyrdom of the young Dr Kotnis was brought alive. Dr Kotnis was sent to war-ridden China at the behest of Jawaharlal Nehru and was part of a medical mission. After some thought, Shantaram took the courageous decision to play the title role himself. His acting, especially towards the end, is heart-rendering and unforgettable.

The second film, *Do Aankhen Barah Haath* (1957), was only appreciated by a few people but is equally impressive. In this film, too, he displayed his acting talent and left a deep impression. Other than this, he employed a unique style of wit and humour, which further heightened the realistic portrayal. His magnificent colour film *Jhanak Payal Baaje* (1955) was conceptualized on a grand scale and soon became a big box office hit. But this student of his, who has drawn inspiration from him from the very beginning, felt that these films were not of much consequence.

However, neither I nor anybody else can deny the fact that despite being over eighty years old, he is still making films with vigour, which is a great inspiration for young people. Upon watching his latest film, *Jal Bin Machhli Nritya Bin Bijli* (1971), I was inspired by his hard work, dedication and admirable direction. He used the newest technique in colour photography and the astounding dance sequences were beautiful. Ordinary films can never match it in its splendour. It seemed like it was something from another world.

Sadly, despite this, the confrontation of social issues and his boldness in doing so is lacking in this film as opposed to his older films, which used to engage with the social ills of the times and boldly bring out societal evils.

However, even though he is over eighty years old, he remains evergreen and with an ever-youthful courage, and in the coming years, we can certainly expect more creativity from him. But (once I had said this in Shantaram's presence) we still hope that classic films like *Duniya Na Mane, Aadmi* and *Padosi* are studied not just by students, but also by filmmakers, including Shantaram himself.

Prithviraj Kapoor: The Shahenshah

It is very difficult for me to write about Prithviraj Kapoor in the past tense. He was a man so full of life, such a vibrant person. It is hard to believe that he is dead. It hurts to recall the times we spent together. I sometimes feel he will suddenly appear, give a whack on my back and say in his unmatched baritone 'What is this, Abbas? What the hell is this? Writing about me in the past tense, as one who is "no more".' Then, in a plaintive tone, these words will roll out: 'Me? Can I ever become was? I will always be is. Never think of me in the past tense.'

To think that I met him fifty years ago. In fact, the first time I 'saw' him, he did not 'see' me. I was returning to Aligarh after spending my holidays in my hometown, Panipat. He was already a star in Calcutta. On the platform of New Delhi Railway Station, somebody pointed out a tall, fair man with a large athletic frame. Dressed in a khaki shirt, pants and Pathani shoes, he was standing in front of the third-class rail compartment.

'Look, look, Prithviraj!'

'Who? The actor?'

'Yes.'

I hadn't seen any of his films. Those were the open air 'bioscope' days. People like me, who lived in small *qasbas*, could rarely see anything other than Westerns. But I had seen his photographs, probably in the magazine *Shabistan*, published from Lahore.

When I reached Aligarh, I proudly told my friends, 'I saw a famous star, not on the screen, but with my own eyes. None other than Prithviraj Kapoor!'

Cherishing this memory, I went to see Debaki Bose's great classic *Seeta* (1934). Later, I boasted before my friends, 'I know the hero; I met him in Delhi.' Tall and beautifully built, the young man was playing Ram. The youth loved him. He was Ram incarnate; like a Greek god who had come to our humble earth. An ordinary dhoti at his waist, his chest proportioned and honed, he was every inch the king. This mythological film was not run-of-the-mill. It evoked unique emotion. Prithviraj had immersed himself in the character in a manner that drew devotion that had never been experienced in Indian cinema. He had distinguished himself from the stars of the day, who were usually long-haired wrestlers, mostly sporting sideburns. He had cast himself into an entirely new mould.

Many stories circulated around this new hero—one that he was MA, LLB; another that he was of noble lineage who had run away from home to work in films; or that he was a married man with several children and had an impeccable character. We both arrived in Bombay around the same time but did not meet until a film event, a debate, brought us face to face. I can't recall what the exact proposition was, but it concerned obscene attacks on film stars. We were arguing hotly. I represented a new crop of film critics but did not realize that 'freedom of press' could be viewed as buying and selling film reviews. I did not anticipate the day when, with cutting-edge photography, we would give birth to a glamour industry. I don't think Prithviraj Kapoor himself realized that his struggle for the dignity and respect of the actor would one day be changed by the very same actors into a saleable item to be traded in black markets.

When I heard his passionate speech at that forum, I was convinced that here existed an actor who was not dependent on a dialogue writer. He beautifully articulated his own ideas. His speech was filled with emotion, and he was able to convey a lot. I also learnt that he respected contrary views. We became good friends.

For many years I observed in Prithviraj Kapoor a beautiful blend of humaneness and stardom. I can confidently say that there was no contradiction in his personality. As is the case with many great artists, his art had merged with his life. One could see his obsession with his art in the way he dressed, his speech and his gestures—it was all theatre. I don't consider this an effort to impress the public; it was grounded in solid reason. Like other greats of the theatre world, a deep sentiment and confidence found expression here. An idealist, he wanted that everything he did onstage or on screen should improve the human condition while, at the same time, reach the highest pinnacle of art.

I can say without a doubt that behind the veil of 'the showman' was a sensitive, honest, idealistic artist who was passionate about improving the lot of his fellow humans. Some people also said that each moment of his life was theatre. While this may be true, but equally true is that all his plays and films were steeped in realism. There was no better expression than his when conveying emotional depth. At the same time, some flaws also crept in because of his total identification with his art. For example, his role of Emperor Akbar in *Mughal-e-Azam* (1960) is a magnificent portrayal of restrained emotion in the tragedy. But the dialogue delivery is overdone, thereby reducing its impact.

But whenever he could present a balance between his conviction and its expression, the result was electrifying. No one, either on stage or screen, has reached that height.

If I were to name two of his masterpieces, I would say Shylock's speech in *Court of Venice* and the title role of Pathan in the eponymous play.

I recall that he delivered the dialogues of Shylock in *Merchant of Venice* from memory before two great screen and stage artists: Russian veterans Nikolai Cherkasov and V.I. Pudovkin. There were no lights, no costumes. Dressed in his usual white kurta pyjama, he just started to speak out the lines from the Shakespeare classic. Everyone there 'saw' a black-cloaked Jew, a victim of racism and hatred, standing in the court of law. And words that had been spoken by innumerable actors in every world language acquired a different life. They became the voice of an oppressed race, the target of insult and abuse. Memories of centuries of pain and humiliation made the lines throb with life, lines that ultimately resulted in the collective revenge of those who were at the receiving end.

Prithvi had played the role with the depths of his being. At the end, he was emotionally spent. I saw Padukan's eyes brimming with tears. Cherkasov embraced him and showered him with kisses. The rest of us, no more than a dozen, were stunned with the force of what we had witnessed.

My number-one choice, however, is Pathan. Very rarely does an actor ascend the stage to perform with the confidence which is born of the collective memory of his generations. Art is thus born, obliterating any difference between the actor and his lived life. It was not only the pinnacle of drama we witnessed, it was also the innocence of youth, bravery of an entire race, folklore of the region. It was their patriotism, their intrepid soldiering. Prithvi had woven all this into his play to make the audience understand and to learn from the Pathans, a learning that was the need of the hour.

I have written several times about him and the characters he played; it has been difficult to separate him from his roles. It would be hard for even a psychologist to say where Prithvi the man started and where Prithvi the artist took over. A man called Prithvi . . . the man and the artist. Everything he did had the flavour of theatre. Whether he was standing outside the theatre, hand outstretched, collecting *chunda* for theatre artists or beating the *naqqara* with peacekeepers while Bombay burnt in communal fires, or dancing in the streets to welcome freedom's dawn—theatre was ubiquitous.

The artist who earned huge amounts spent it all in establishing progressive, idealistic, Hindustani theatre. Not only was it a financial drain, it was also a setback to his health. All this apart, he gained phenomenal success and it can be said that while his persona was that of a showman, his personality was that of an idealist, indeed a ghazi in its best definition.

So many aspects of his life come to mind. Struggling stage artist, top hero of Indian cinema, successful stage and film producer, one flop-film producer, untiring social activist, determined fund raiser and proud father of three sons who walked in his footsteps to the pinnacle of success. He was also member of Parliament, a role in which he could not shine since his heart was elsewhere! But, above all, he was the flagbearer of forgotten values.

He had friends in many circles: Congress workers, socialists, communists. From Kashmir to Kerala, his admirers were everywhere. Outside India, Peking and Moscow rang with his praise.

He was sought after in government circles. But he valued his personal freedom, and no matter what he was offered, he never compromised with state imperatives. He was ever-ready to stand for a social cause, never caring for repercussions. This principle of his life tremendously helped the progressive movement, and sometimes even non-progressives took advantage of his commitment. Being an idealist, he was unconcerned with profit and loss in such matters. He was an artist, not a social scientist. He was lover of his *watan*, not a politician. He was a reformer, not a revolutionary, and above all an actor, not a leader.

If only anyone opened the treasure house of memories!

To encapsulate his personality, his virtues, his achievements in one article is trying to capture an ocean in a goblet . . .

One last word. There was only one Prithviraj. But he can never be 'was'. He will always be 'is'. He is eternal; to conflate him with death is to show him disrespect.

Raj Kapoor: An Extraordinary Karmayogi

I watched Mehboob Khan's film *Andaz* (1949) and, a few days later, wrote the story of *Awara* (1951). I suggested to Mehboob Khan that both Prithviraj Kapoor and Raj Kapoor should be cast in the film.

Although Mehboob Khan was keen to cast Prithviraj Kapoor, he preferred to have Dilip Kumar play the hero instead of Raj Kapoor. I did not agree with that. During those days, Raj Kapoor was on the lookout for a script. He had acted in only one film prior to this—*Aag* (1948). When he found out that I had written a story and suggested his name to Mehboob Khan for the central character, he approached me.

In those days, Raj was quite down to earth, with no vanity. When he came to me, I told him the story of *Awara.*

In my mind, Raj Kapoor is like an engine, and I felt that if this engine could be connected to the right vehicle, it would spread my views far and wide. This is the reason I write for him, despite knowing that he makes some modifications; so do I. No matter what he does, through him, I know that my thoughts and words will, in some form or the other, have a wide reach.

In *Awara,* he did not alter as much, but in *Shree 420 (1955),* he altered a bit more, and by the time *Bobby (1973)* was released, I had to say this was not my film, it belonged to Raj Kapoor. My story was about the relationship between a rich boy and a poor girl. There was an ayah, who was transformed into a governess by Raj Kapoor. He placed a refrigerator in her house, stocked with liquor. I had depicted the girl's father as being poor, but Raj Kapoor showed him to be a rich fisherman with money in his safe!

Despite all this, Raj Kapoor is a powerful engine who enables me to communicate my thoughts. This is the reason why I allowed him to place money in the fisherman's safe.

When Nargis was being cast as the heroine in *Awara,* she objected that the role was not significant enough and was unwilling to play it. She said, 'There is no role for me in *Awara.*' I told her, 'I understand that there is no role for you in *Awara,* but I will write another story just for you.' And so, I made *Anhonee* (1952), in which the role was specially written for Nargis. Nargis agreed to work in *Awara* only after listening to in the script of *Anhonee.* Both *Awara* and *Anhonee* were shot simultaneously.

I have known Raj Kapoor for the past twenty-five years, from the time when he was not known as Raj Kapoor but simply as 'Raju' or 'Prithviraj's elder son'. At that time, this plump, fair-skinned boy used to be a clapper boy for Bombay Talkies' films and would always be on the lookout to play any small role.

He would travel in the third-class compartment of the Bombay local from Malad to Dadar and was an assistant to his famous father at Prithvi Theatre, where he would do the set design for plays and even perform some small comic roles in productions like *Shakuntala* and *Deewar*.

I have known him since his first film, *Aag*. He would run from one end of Bombay to the to the other to get Rs 1000 to make his film or even for a can of film stock.

While making his second film, *Barsaat*, he would sometimes doze off in his second-hand car after wrapping up the shooting. On other occasions, he would sit cross-legged on the floor along with his entire staff, eating food bought from some restaurant on Grant Road.

One evening, while shooting *Awara*, his accountant informed him that all the funds given by [one] 'MG' were exhausted and there was no money left to continue. That same night, Raj decided to shoot the dream sequence that took three months and Rs 3 lakh. I was with him on the night when *Awara* premiered in Moscow and the audience applauded him for ten minutes. After that night, Raj became the most loved film hero of the Soviet people.

I have seen Raj through his various moods. I've seen him laugh and make others laugh. I have seen him sing, cry, drink and get other people drunk. I have seen him beat the dhol and dance with abandon.

I have also heard all sorts of things about him. Some say that he is the best actor in India, others feel he is just a jester, a joker. Some say he is large-hearted, while others say he does not have a heart at all. Some say Raj is an actor who keeps acting even in real life and others say he is a 'flirt' and a 'philanderer' who gets involved with every new actress. There are several rumours that run rife about him being in love with someone or the other.

But I know for a fact (as do the people who know him closely) that Raj has only one abiding and true love—himself.

Raj believes in every manifestation of God. There is an idol of Lord Shiva outside his studio, a picture of Jesus Christ in his cottage along with inscriptions from the Quran, a statue of Mahatma Buddha and that of Sai Baba but, above all these, he believes in himself and his soul.

Raj Kapoor is most interested in Raj Kapoor. If he is interested in other people, it is only by virtue of their association with Raj Kapoor, which means that he is interested in the Soviet Union because his films are extremely popular there. He is interested in the art of filmmaking because he makes films. If it were up to him, he would not watch nor let anyone watch films not made by him.

In Raj Kapoor's dictionary, the most important word is 'I'. He wishes to make a film titled *Mera Naam Joker* (1970). After that he is planning another, *Main Aur Mera Dost*. Who is this 'dost', this friend? It is him, his own spirit. It must be a story about a man and his inner self—the story of Raj Kapoor and Raju.

So, why do his friends and companions tolerate his self-love? If he only loves himself then why do we all love him? This is because he does, in fact, love something more than himself, and that is his work, his art.

He can sacrifice anything in the world in order to make a good film—money, time, comfort, even happiness, his own as well as that of others. He forgets everything while working, including his wife, children, friends and relatives, and works tirelessly like one possessed.

He works like a madman, not like a lunatic in an institution but like Majnun, who is enraptured. He is like Farhad, who, through the chisel of his art, wants to cut through mountains of gold and make rivulets of milk flow through them (but on the condition that there should be a sign on the shore that proclaims that this rivulet has been forged by Raj Kapoor).

This self-love and belief in himself, however, is not just some ordinary arrogance. It is the vanity of Narcissus, who fell in love with his own reflection when he saw it in water. It is not selfishness but self-confidence which, when elevated to a higher plane, becomes a defining philosophy of life.

If it is true that work is worship, then Raj Kapoor is an extraordinary karmayogi of the twentieth century. The degree of his dedication and involvement with his art is at par with the highest form of love proclaimed by Sufi saints. The only difference being that a Sufi or a true believer can separate his soul from his work and lose his soul in the *paramatma*.

For an artist, his self-belief is like a powerful engine that can thrust him forward at great speed. But unless it is fuelled by principles and grounded to the rails of humanity, that engine will keep wandering aimlessly on the tracks of vanity.

The day Raj Kapoor's 'I' is subsumed within the 'Us' of humanity, that day his work, his art and his *karmayog* will reach the pinnacle of success.

Dilip Kumar: Loss of a National Treasure

Dilip Kumar has many virtues and one of them is his frankness.

After watching the premiere of *Gyara Hazar Ladkian* (1962), he asked me a question in front of a crowd of people, 'Abbas Sahib, why did you make this inane film?'

I answered, 'I made a mistake. It won't happen in the future!' I didn't say this out of any complaint or humility. Though I had directed the film, I agreed with his opinion. In *Gyara Hazar Ladkian,* I was unable to say what I really wanted to and, as a result, could not make the film I really wanted to. The art and objective of the film were sacrificed due to my immoderate pursuit of box-office success. In the end, I was neither here nor there.

I was determined not to repeat my mistake, and one year later, I made *Shehar aur Sapna* (1963). The film was regarded as one of the best made that year and won the President's Gold Medal. But Dilip Kumar could not find the time to watch the film. He was perhaps busy shooting for inane films like *Leader* (1964) or *Dil Diya Dard Liya* (1966).

Among my many flaws, one is that of being frank, and now, I want to ask Dilip Kumar the same question that he asked me in front of so many people, 'Dilip Sahib, why are you making these inane films—*Azaad* (1955), *Kohinoor* (1960), *Leader*, *Dil Diya Dard Liya*?'

I would not pose this question to any other actor, but I will ask him. This is because I adore and respect him and also admire his talent and artistic perfection.

But by working in one mindless film after another, Dilip Kumar is stifling that outstanding artist. If someone does not stop him from doing so, it is possible that an exceptional actor will be sacrificed at a gilded altar. It will be an big tragedy if that happens. In some cases, like in the case of *Shaheed* (1948), a murder can be pardoned, and sometimes, like in the case of *Devdas* (1955), a suicide is understandable, but when murder and suicide are brought together, it is inexcusable.

So, I repeat my question to him, 'Why are you making these inane films—*Azaad, Kohinoor, Leader, Dil Diya Dard Liya, Ram aur Shyam* (1967)?'

By inane I do not mean to indicate that they have not fared well commercially. Out of these four films, two were hits while the other two flopped.

By inane I mean useless, dishonest, substandard films lacking in artistic credibility. It doesn't matter whether they earned Rs 2 lakh at the box office or Rs 2 crore, whether they ran for two weeks or two years.

I am posing this question to Dilip Kumar because his talent is a national treasure. We take pride in him as Indians, as through his talent, he can enhance the character and culture of our nation. Even he does not have the right to waste it.

Once again, I repeat my question: 'Why are you making these inane films?'

I am asking you this question (and not your so-called producers) because you take on the responsibility of each aspect of your films—from the choice of story to the dialogues, setting, costumes and even editing. You work for months, sometimes years, on a script; supervise every aspect of the film; and without your approval a film cannot be released. You fulfil the responsibilities of a producer, director, actor and writer yourself.

Are you making such films because you need the money? Do you think only such films will yield profit?

Are you making these films because you think you will attain fame and popularity through them or do you genuinely think that these films are good just because the audience likes them and you wish to please your fans? Pleasing the audience is the dominion of a politician, not an artist. A true artist does not blindly pander to the demands of the people. What he offers them speaks to their soul and emotions. If a diseased person or madman asks you for poison, will you promptly hand it to him?

Your fame and popularity are no less today than it was before *Azaad* (1955).

The world witnessed your craft in films such as *Milan* (1946), *Shaheed*, *Andaz* (1949), *Musafir*, *Devdas*, *Mughal-e-Azam* (1960), as it was being honed and sculpted in every film. It seemed that this beloved artist of ours would pluck the stars from the sky and reach the very heights of artistic excellence.

But then *Azaad* came and instead of an emotionally stirring performance and intense characterization, we saw an inferior imitation done by an impersonator. Instead of a film script, we saw a nautanki, where you put on a beard and played a doctor; you dressed up as Radha and wielded tin swords . . . Although an impersonator is also an artist and nautanki an art form, it isn't comparable to the calibre at which Dilip Kumar's exceptional acting once was. Such films may have brought him cheap fame and admiration but at what price? The price of an artist being auctioned off in the marketplace?

I do not share any hostility towards entertaining films like *Azaad* or *Ram aur Shyam* but such characters can easily be played by an ordinary comedian. To give an artist like Dilip Kumar such roles is akin to using a gun to kill a fly or asking an eminent musician like Ravi Shankar to play in a wedding band just because he will be paid lakhs of rupees for it!

By acting in films like *Gunga Jumna* (1961) and *Mughal-e-Azam*, you have yourself proved that instead of superficial roles of fun and frolic, you prefer emotional stories and serious characters. You are a man of good taste and are well educated. People admire your balanced temperament, manners and etiquette.

Then why do you work in these inane films?

There is only one other reason. It seems you are making artistically worthless films that are just mindless entertainment in order to make money. But this allure cannot be just for money. Whether you earn 1 lakh or 10 lakh, after a point, wealth too becomes meaningless. Today, money is considered a status symbol and an artist is considered big or small depending on the fee that he commands. Do you agree?

Was the Dilip Kumar of *Devdas* and *Gunga Jumna* a lesser artist, and has the Dilip Kumar of *Ram aur Shyam* become a bigger artist because his fee has gone up? Will art now be valued in terms of money? There are so many other parameters to assess you!

For the past few years, why has no film of yours won a National Award? Have you ever given this a thought? There was a time when you were working with the most exceptional directors of India, but not anymore. You worked with Bimal Roy in films like *Devdas* and *Madhumati* (1958), made a meaningful and pragmatic film like *Musafir* (1957) with Hrishikesh Mukherjee and worked with B.R. Chopra in *Naya Daur* (1957). Why are you no longer working with directors of that stature or even those better than them? Is it not a fact that ever since your fee has increased, you have extracted yourself from the circle of rational, artistic, progressive filmmakers simply because they cannot afford to pay so much? Nor will they allow you to interfere with their creativity and vision.

We want to see a distinguished artist like you in films made by distinguished directors so that their art and your artistry come together to forge an exceptional film. Everybody requires money, especially film artists and producers, but not to such an extent that they are willing to compromise on their artistic standards.

Paul Muni was an accomplished theatre and film artist in Hollywood (you too must have admired him). He once asked his wife how much money she would need to live comfortably. She replied that for their family $1000 per month was enough. At that, Paul Muni said, 'Then why am I working in silly films and plays and compromising my artistic standards?'

Thereon, he only worked in films and theatre productions that would complement his craft. Whether he was paid more money or less (and it was mostly less), he did not make compromises with shoddy art ever again.

You earned more money than the president and prime minister of India by working on *Shaheed, Azaad* and *Devdas*. How did a serious man and great artist like you get entwined in this blind race for money that has taken over the world, especially the film world?

Irrespective of whose name appears as the producer, it is a commonly known fact that you have been producing your films. For the past few years, you have also been directing your films and contributing significantly towards the scenes, story and dialogues. So, you know that for a film to come together, there needs to be a meeting of the minds where several talented people collaborate.

Dilip Kumar alone cannot make an exceptional film. Raj Kapoor alone cannot create an exceptional film. One exceptional artist (be it Paul Muni or Chandramohan) can't make an exceptional film by himself.

A serious, meaningful, moving and dramatic story is needed to bring out the remarkable skill of an artist. You need someone who is well-versed with the finer nuances of writing to write a competent screenplay. Similarly, for dialogues, you need a litterateur who is knowledgeable about idioms, phrases, wordplay, and can write dialogues accordingly. You need someone with a skilled and creative mind to direct the film and a notable cameraman who, through his interplay of light and shadows, colours and patterns, infuses the film with life.

Apart from acting, you might be interested in different film departments and might even be as accomplished a director as an actor. Raj Kapoor, Sunil Dutt and Manoj Kumar are a few examples, yet to work in other departments you need to be suitably proficient in those fields, so that you can be as adept at them as you are in your acting.

Did you learn nothing from the experience of making *Leader* or *Dil Diya Dard Liya*?

I remember a conversation when you had asked me, 'Abbas Sahib, how long does it take you to write a script?'

I had replied, 'If I am not working on anything else, then I can have the first draft of a script ready in one month.'

And you had replied that you (and your producer) had been working on one scene for the past month but were still not satisfied with it.

On hearing this, I had said, 'If you make me stand in front of the camera with make-up on my face, it will take me one month just to figure out that we've been doing multiple takes of the first scene alone!'

With a degree of astonishment, you had asked, 'What do you mean?'

I had replied, 'I mean that a person should do what he knows best.'

In the end, I wish to reiterate that you are among the two great actors of India (the other being Raj Kapoor). You portray characters with emotional flair and can play sophisticated comic roles as well. There is no one who can rival you in dialogue delivery. With these qualities you can work in and create significant films provided you realize your artistic responsibility with fervour. And for God's sake, do not waste your expertise (which you have honed with your hard work and intelligence) on meaningless stories and inane films.

> *Rakhiyo 'Ghalib' mujhe, iss talkh nawa i mein muaaf*
> *aaj kuch dard mere dil mein siwa hota hai*
> *Forgive me Ghalib if I speak with bitterness*
> *Today my heart aches more than ever before*

Meena Kumari: The Muse, the Ghazal

It was twelve years ago, the first day of the shoot of *Char Dil Char Rahein* (1959). It had been raining all night, for twelve hours non-stop. I have a principle: On the day of the shoot, I reach the studio very early in the morning. That day too I managed to reach Modern Studio at an early hour. The roads were flooded. The taxi on the road was like a boat on a river. At one point the driver had to stop because water had seized the engine. He was able to start it somehow and it reached the studio gates. But he refused to take it inside as the road inside the compound was invisible. It had turned into a huge lake. I rolled my trousers up to my knees, removed my shoes and stepped into the water.

I was drenched to the bone when I entered the studio. A fire had been lit to dry it. None of my assistants had arrived. Only Pandari Jurak, the make-up artist, had spread out his wares in the make-up room.

Pandari said, 'Abbas Sahib, you will have to cancel the shoot today. No heroine will leave her house on a day like this.'

I said, 'This is the first day of the shoot; it will be a test for the heroine!'

Pandari asked, 'What time did you give them?'

'7.30 because the shoot starts at 9.30 and it takes two hours to put on "black" make-up.'

He looked at his watch, 'It is 7.30 already.'

Right at that moment, the sound of a horn sounded through the pitter-patter and a car 'sailed' up the stairs, most of which were immersed in water, of the make-up room.

First appeared a pair of small, dainty bare feet; then a pair of hands dangling sandals; then a form in a white sari, head covered in a white towel. She walked freely through the standing water into the make-up room.

'*Adab*, Abbas Sahib. Hope I am not late?' she said as she sat before the mirror. 'I have learnt my dialogues. You have written them so well, I had no difficulty. But how does an untouchable Haryanvi girl speak? That you will have to teach me.' That was the heroine of the film, Meena Kumari. People say she is dead, she has left this world. But she is vividly alive today . . . in many memories I treasure.

There were three heroines in *Char Dil Char Rahein*—Meena Kumari, Nimmi and Kumkum. Each one did full justice to the character she played but everyone in our unit called Meena Kumari 'Heroine Number One'; she will always be called so. Why? Maybe because she did not look or behave like a heroine at all. She never dressed flashily like other film stars; a white voile saree was her favourite attire. She was never capricious nor did she put on airs like some other film stars. She always memorized her dialogues before arriving on the sets. She would never ask, 'Which scene are we shooting today?' or 'Oh! I forgot my dialogue sheet at home.'

Everyone—from the producer to the assistant make-up artist, even the camera coolie—was happy with her because she treated everyone with sympathy and simplicity. She did not try to teach direction to the director, she did not try to explain camera angles to the photographer. As soon as the camera was switched on, she got lost in her character. She was no longer Meena Kumari; she would become the character she was portraying. When I narrated the story of *Char Dil Char Rahein* to her and Kamal Amrohi, her husband and my long-time friend, my heartfelt wish was that she should play the character of Chavli, the *chamarin*. But I said to her, 'You can choose any character you like to play. The first choice is yours, the other heroines will choose later. After hearing the story, she immediately said, 'I would like to play the role of Chavli chamarin!' Kamal Amrohi smiled and said, 'In fact, the character is tailor-made for you. But as Abbas Sahib says the precondition is that you will have to apply make-up to look like Chavli.' She said simply, 'That is inevitable. That is exactly why I have chosen to enact this one.'

Meena Kumari and Chavali chamarin! The actress and the person! The juxtaposition was day and night, sky and earth, complete contrasts. One was a popular actress, the other an untouchable chamarin who made a living by selling dung cakes. One was called Mahjabeen (moon-faced) because of her fair skin and flawless beauty, the other was 'dark as dark can be, the darkest of them all!' One was a reader of books, reciter of couplets, herself a poet, the other an unlettered rustic and an untouchable!

Would Meena Kumari, the fair, educated, sophisticated actress be able to play the unlettered, rustic, dark-skinned chamarin? I had no doubt in my mind that she would. But many of my friends and family were afraid that Meena Kumari would remain Meena Kumari 'the star' and would never be able to look or sound low caste.

From the very first day, when she emerged from her make-up room, wearing coarse garments and cheap ornaments, she completely transformed into Chavli. From that day onwards, she stopped sitting on the heroine's chair. She would sit on a broken charpoy or cross-legged on a tattered rug on the floor as if in a village *chaupal*.

On the first day of the shoot of *Char Dil Char Rahein,* someone came to meet her. He stood right in front of her and asked, 'Hasn't Meena ji come yet?' I said well, you know, heroines don't come on time, but if you want to talk to Chavli, she is sitting right in front of you!' At this point, Chavli suddenly broke into peals of laughter and the ruse was discovered. Such mix-ups often happened on the sets.

It is said of every film star that he or she gets fully lost and engrossed in his or her role, but how far was it true of Meena Kumari? I can vouch for it, everybody in my unit can and so could the burnt soles of her feet!

It was the month of May. The sun was at its peak on a hot burning afternoon. We were shooting in a stone quarry near Andheri. Hundreds of labourers were toiling, breaking the burning stones. Among them were film artists and extras for the crowd scenes. Everyone was complaining of heat and thirst; they asked for ice water again and again and refused to shoot barefoot on the burning rocks. Among them was Meena Kumari but when she came out of her car, she was barefoot.

'Please wear your sandals when we shoot the close-up scenes,' I suggested.

'Sandals! Poor Chavli. How could she ever dream of wearing sandals? Would she have come to the quarry to break stones if she had sandals?' she asked.

I was speechless. When I touched the stone, it was burning. So, I took off my shoes and socks. The cameraman took off his chappals. Every assistant director and all unit hands removed their footwear. The whole day Chavli kept walking and running on the burning stones, kept breaking stones with the heavy chisel and hammer. Meena Kumari remained barefoot even when we took a lunch break. She never told anyone what happened to those delicate feet by the evening, but none of us has forgotten to this day how our feet were burnt, blistered, bruised and bloodied.

So, this was Meena Kumari on whose death the whole film industry and thousands of fans shed tears. She was in love with her art and passionate about it, a passion that bordered on insanity. Her passion was both her ailment and her remedy. Seven years before her death, a renowned London specialist had diagnosed a failing liver and given her just one year to live. But she continued to live, fighting her illness. It was only when *Pakeezah* (1972) and several other projects in the pipeline were completed that she surrendered to the angel of death. She left the world at the age of forty.

She worked tirelessly. Whether the film was small or big, the director famous or unknown, she worked with full dedication and commitment. She could infuse life into the weakest of scripts with her flawless acting. Even then, out of the seventy-eight films she acted in, only a dozen or so can be called masterpieces. Her last film, *Pakeezah*, will remain one of the most memorable. The fact is that an artist individually can do very little to raise the level of a film. There are several factors which collectively contribute to make a film into a work of art. In our country, ninety out of a hundred films are of very poor quality. Everyone knows this; so did Meena Kumari. But whenever she got a chance to demonstrate her talent, she excelled.

This was Meena Kumari, the famous film star on whose name films sold and big crowds gathered in front of cinema halls. But there was another Meena Kumari hiding inside.

There is a Russian doll called the matryoshka; another doll is hidden inside this doll. Many dolls are hidden inside one another. Similarly, there were many Meena Kumaris inside one another. One Meena Kumari was the actress who acted not to earn money or fame or adulation, but because it gave her peace of mind and satisfied her inner soul. Then there was the sensitive poet, one who secretly wrote poems for the fulfilment of her aching, restless soul. She recorded these poems only in her last days in her own voice for posterity. Hidden in these many layers was a little girl named Mahjabeen who had spent her childhood in dismal poverty. Who, like all girls, wanted to play with dolls, wanted to sit on a *hindola*, get married and have children. But family circumstances were such that she was forced to bury all her small dreams and aspirations at the tender age of seven and work as a child artist to support her entire family.

Today, when she is no more, I imagine that all her life Meena Kumari kept searching for this little Mahjabeen. This innocent girl was always within her. God only knows how many dreams, aspirations and desires she nursed. Maybe the restlessness of her soul, the poetry behind her drinking, her bitter-sweet smile, the depth, sobriety and restraint in her acting were the results of this search. But today that search is over. In death Meena Kumari and Mahjabeen have become one.

Only the story remains and a few beautiful memories.

Balraj Sahni: The People's Artist

In our country, unfortunately, famous painters, actors and musicians are not bestowed with the title of 'people's artists'. They are only made to queue up alongside engineers, doctors, businessmen, social workers and other such people and given awards like the Padma Shri and Padma Bhushan. Consequently, tribute is often not paid to their distinguished creative work and exceptional talent.

The one who is most deserving of this title is Balraj Sahni. He dedicated a significant part of his life to freeing the stage and screen from their purely commercial moorings and assimilating common life and reality within it. People really liked the way he was able to portray varied characters from ordinary life with great ease. The landless farmer in *Dharti ke Lal* (1946), the depressed and unemployed young man in *Hum Log* (1951), the rickshaw puller in *Do Bigha Zamin* (1953), the dry fruit seller in *Kabuliwala* (1961) are a few examples, along with the characters he later played on the stage, which included Mirza Ghalib in the play *Aakhri Shama* by the Indian People's Theatre Association

(IPTA). These characters are a distillation of his minute and profound study of common people and weave in the essence of life itself. But not many people know the difficulties with which he incorporated these characterizations.

Balraj Sahni was not born in an opulent home; he was appreciative of the common life which he had experienced through his involvement and participation in people's movements, various protests and demonstrations for social justice, even facing the batons and bullets of the police. Maxim Gorky said, 'Life is a university', and Balraj Sahni was educated at this university and completed his higher studies through his experiences in prison. He thought of common people and their lives as a source of boundless knowledge and continued to be immersed in its study.

IPTA was established during World War II and the Bengal famine and Balraj Sahni was among its founder members. As an actor and director, he executed several functions. But as a field worker, his work was beyond compare as he assiduously accomplished several tasks for IPTA without any expectations or greed.

He was a methodical organizer and part of each of IPTA's missions—whether it was a war against fascism or efforts to maintain Hindu–Muslim unity in the face of communal riots or a movement for African independence or the war in Vietnam against imperial powers. He not only lent wholehearted emotional support but would also motivate people to be part of the movements. He worked with such a fervent drive during the riots that it almost seemed like he was being driven by some inner force. He would write plays and offer guidance to people like me to write as well. He would rehearse for the plays and present them on busy streets, along chawls and pavements, at

Chowpatty and sometimes even in halls. (My play *Zubeida* was directed by him. While it was being staged at Cowasji Jehangir Hall, he brought an entire wedding procession, complete with the band and the groom sitting atop a horse, which made its way to the stage.)

He achieved many accolades in films which cannot be overlooked, and portrayed every character in an exceedingly realistic manner.

In 1945, IPTA completed *Dharti ke Lal* with the assistance of several new and non-professional actors. At the time, this tall, well-built actor had just returned to India after spending two years at the British Broadcasting Corporation (BBC) in England, and was given a role to play—one of the many characters plagued by hunger due to the famine.

In order to convincingly portray a malnourished person, he ate just one meal a day for several months. On the day of the shoot, before coming in front of the camera, he smeared mud all over himself, his dhoti and even his face, so that he looked the part.

Bimal Roy's internationally acclaimed film *Do Bigha Zamin* portrays the plight of a poor rickshaw puller who struggles to pay off his debt to the moneylender and free his land of two bighas from his clutches. In order to fully understand and internalize the character, Sahni stayed in the hutments of rickshaw pullers for several weeks. Not only did he learn to pull the rickshaw, he also skilfully adopted their mannerisms and appearance.

The most famous scene of the film is one where he takes on a fat passenger and races with a horse-drawn carriage just to earn a reward of mere Rs 10, and wins. Bimal Roy told me that, for the long shot, he had planned to film a real rickshaw

puller who would be wearing the same clothes as Balraj Sahni.
But Sahni did not agree to this at all and, in fact, executed
the scene in an exceedingly realistic manner, not allowing any
'double' to interfere with it. So much so, he even put his life
in danger while running and gave an unforgettable shot—a
shining example of realistic acting. The film highlighted social
causes pertaining to the underprivileged, and his portrayal of
the character reinforced his talent and proved that he truly was
an exceptional actor. With it, he also won the hearts of crores of
labourers and workers, and with tremendous love and respect
became known as the people's actor.

Based on Rabindranath Tagore's exceptional work, the
film *Kabuliwala* saw Sahni play the role of a fair-complexioned
pathan. The character reminded him of his own childhood
spent in Rawalpindi, and he recalled the friendly Pathans from
a border province in Pakistan whom he had met.

For the role, Sahni contacted some local Pathans so that he
could learn their ways, dialect, mannerisms and defining traits.
He even learnt to sing Pashto songs in their distinct accent.

He portrayed the role with such conviction that wherever
he travelled, people welcomed him by imitating the mannerisms
of 'Kabuliwala' from the film.

His other great achievement lay in the context of the stage,
in the play *Aakhri Shama* by IPTA, in which he brought Mirza
Ghalib to life. Unfortunately, the dream of bringing this play
to the big screen could not be realized but the people who
watched it deeply appreciated his performance.

Although Balraj Sahni (a proud Punjabi) was proficient in
Urdu, he wanted to grasp the particular manner in which Ghalib
would speak Urdu, so that he could master the character. This
he learnt from his friends in Delhi.

Apart from this, he even learnt how to recite couplets like an expert, in the way they are recited at *mushairas*. He played this character in such a realistic and compelling manner that a scholar of Ghalib remarked that even though he had not met the poet, he knew for sure that Ghalib must have looked like Balraj Sahni, must have read poetry like the actor and even reacted in the manner that was portrayed.

One gets an idea of the actor and his craft when one sees the ways in which he presents each character. Balraj's other memorable characters include that of the Anglo-Indian doctor from the film *Rahi* (1953), the jailor in the film *Hulchul* (1951), the tamasha wallah from *Pardesi* (1957), who travels from one place to another to perform, the runaway criminal from *Pinjre ke Panchhi* (1966), a magnanimous person who becomes an alcoholic in *Daaman aur Aag* (1973), the wealthy businessman in *Pyar ka Rishta* (1973), the police inspector from *Hanste Zakhm* (1973), and his last film *Garm Hawa* (1973), which was released after his death. It is an issue-based, political film in which he plays a Muslim shoe manufacturer in Agra whose business is completely destroyed in the wake of the communal riots that erupted after Partition. Despite this, he is unwilling to leave his country and go to Pakistan. Balraj left an imprint on each of these varied characters. His talent was honed not only through a deep study of the human mind and emotions, but also by minutely scrutinizing the actions and mannerisms of people with a lot of depth and compassion.

He was not trained at any film institute and had, in fact, studied English literature. Naturally, the question arises— where did he learn the craft of acting? The answer is: in the school of life where he learnt to closely observe the behaviour, strengths and weaknesses of people. He studied their style, mannerisms and even the particular cut of their clothes. It must have certainly been an exceptional school as his experiences brought him so many accomplishments.

After completing his master's in English literature from Government College, Lahore, he spent one year at Rabindranath Tagore's Shantiniketan, during which time he became familiar with Bengal's artistic, aesthetic and creative films, and absorbed the culture. After that, he lived for some time at the Gandhi ashram in Wardha and campaigned for basic education for all. During this time he lived a simple and disciplined life like the rest of the residents at the ashram. Lionel Fielden, who was a great supporter of India, had become the director-general of All India Radio. He got Sahni a job and, during the time of World War II, Sahni lived in London and broadcast the news, plays and interviews for BBC. While in London, he was fascinated by the writings of Karl Marx, and he returned to India determined to dedicate his entire life to the service of ordinary people; it was then that he became a member of the Communist Party of India.

He also became associated with IPTA and threw himself headlong into acting, directing and presenting plays on the stage. However, these plays were not staged in air-conditioned theatres but on the fine sands of Chowpatty, sometimes in dirty slums where the makeshift stage would be constructed by placing four tables together and the audience would be seated on the road.

Later, he (and I) started presenting our plays in theatres, taking up important contemporary issues. However, performing inside theatres did not alter our mission towards humanity, neither did it sever our ties with the common people because we had devoted our lives to the common people and culture. This was how dedicated and passionate he was towards his work. He was not a superficial communist party worker. He was rational, agnostic and had the courage to see all of his endeavours through.

When his daughter passed away, he was busy campaigning for the Congress Party in a remote area in Madhya Pradesh. In Bhiwandi, when communal riots broke out, he stayed in a Muslim-dominated area for two weeks so he could build their confidence in a secular India. He kept travelling to different parts of India, engaging in some good cause or another. He was not only writing plays for IPTA and the Juhu Art Theatre but also directing them, acting in them and, in fact, would even contribute funds to stage the plays. The money he earned from his films went towards the humanitarian causes he had taken on as his life's mission. When I met him just a few weeks before his death, he was contemplating building a hostel for Indian and Arab students, in which the students could stay together. I spoke with him on the phone just one hour before he passed away due to a heart attack. He told me he had been thinking about building a memorial hospital in Hyderabad.

He actively participated in the people's struggle and this experience imbued his distinctive personality with a certain quality. This in turn enabled him to bring forth the real passion of human emotions in the different characters he portrayed.

Besides being an exceptional actor, he was a story writer as well. He would write in Hindi and later wrote in his beloved language Punjabi, and worked with love and dedication for its advancement.

After completing a two-week-long tour of Pakistan, he wrote an exceptional travelogue that was appreciated by people in both India and Pakistan. This was such an extraordinary achievement. He was extremely fond of Punjab—its language, culture and the mannerisms of the people. This is why he could win over the heart of any Punjabi who came from Lahore. When one young editor from Lahore came to India as part of a friendly tour, Balraj hosted a dinner party for him and there he proclaimed his desire for all Punjabis to unite and come together. Although he loved the Punjabi language, like Pandit Nehru, he too was in favour of adopting the Roman script for various Indian languages for the sake of national unity. Sometimes he would write letters to his near and dear friends in Roman Hindustani. Whenever he would go for shoots to the studio, he would take his Gurmukhi typewriter along with him, on which he would write essays, stories, plays or novels during his lunch break. All these works would be published in Punjabi.

While shooting *Garm Hawa* in Agra, he would spend his free time with the Muslim craftsmen to learn from them. This was because he was playing this role in the film. If he would be shooting in some village in Punjab, he would spend the evening among the villagers there and record their conversations and songs so that he could enrich his knowledge and vocabulary and mould his dialect and body language to bring authenticity to his character.

He was in love with art and progressive thought in literature, plays and film. He was fond of Russia, China, Vietnam, Cuba and the Arab countries but, above all, he was in love with the people of India. He assimilated their lives and their struggles, their issues, weaknesses and strengths, within himself.

This is why his last words, befittingly, were, 'Give my love to my people.'

Amitabh Bachchan: Himmatwala

AMITABH = Alif, Meem, Ye, Te, Alif, Bhe

Alif for Allah, Alif for Ishwar, Alif for Amitabh. Meem for Mohd Manohar Musalman, Mast Maula, Maut (death), which he almost embraced. Ye for Yaari, ye for Yes Sir. In the alphabet ye is the last letter. Te for Throne on which Amitabh sits. Te also for Taj even if it is made of fake diamonds because it is a filmi crown which Amitabh 'was' wearing and 'is' wearing. Alif also for Anwar Ali, which was his first film character in *Saat Hindustani* (1969). Bhe for Bhai (brother), Amitabh's brother Ajitabh who is younger, but when the actor was sick proved himself as the elder. Bhe also for Bhalai (goodness)—all the good deeds Amitabh has done, which came in handy during those tough times.

Amitabh and my personal story began by coincidence. It is wrongly said that he came to me with a letter from Indira Gandhi. This may have happened with another producer. One

day his younger brother came to me with Jalal Agha. At the
time I was selecting artists for my film *Saat Hindustani*.

Jalal said, 'Mamujan, this is Ajitabh. He does not want a
role in films, but he has a photograph which you may like to see
and thus get the seventh Hindustani you are looking for. We
can then begin shooting the film.'

I said, 'Let's look at this one too.' I used to see eight to ten
photos every day. So I had very little hope of finding a suitable
face. I glanced casually at the photo; it was demi-sized but there
was something there which made me look again, carefully. First,
the boy was very tall; second, his eyes were beautiful; third,
he was wearing the clothes I wanted this character to wear:
churidar pyjamas, kurta and Jawahar jacket.

I had no idea who he was where he was from or whose son
he was! Was he educated or was he a 'matric fail'? 'I will meet
him day after tomorrow.' (The next day I had to write *Last Page*
and *Azad Qalam* for *Blitz*.)

Jalal's friend said, 'Fine, Sir, he will be here.' I thought he
was from Bombay.

'I will wait for him until then . . . but no longer. Because this
is why the film is stuck!'

'The boy will be here,' Jalal's friend assured me.

On the appointed day, the young man stood before me.
Tall, thin, fair and shy. I took one look at him . . . Anwar Ali,
just as I had imagined him. I asked, 'When can you start work?'

'Work?' he was startled. But his voice had a fine timbre,
sounded good. 'At once.' 'But,' I said disclosing all the facts.

'This film has seven heroes; the seventh is, in fact, a heroine.
We can't give more than Rs 5000 to anyone—neither the
seniors nor the juniors.'

'I agree,' the boy said. 'But won't you take any tests?'

'No, we don't take tests.'

'I have the results of three or four tests. Should I show them to you?'

'No. I don't want to see others' tests. By the way, who took these tests?' He named four famous producers (if I reveal their names, it would be an insult).

I said, 'In any case, I don't take tests; I take the artist on face value.'

He smiled; an innocent look. The smile then extended to his eyes. 'I didn't understand . . . other producers took repeated tests, including dialogue delivery tests. They measured me, weighed me.'

'And then?' I asked.

'Rejected. They said I was too tall, too ungainly, looked like a caricature and no heroine would want to work with me.'

'This is irrelevant for me. I have six heroes, one heroine, and she is new. I have found the boy I was looking for.'

'Found?' he repeated my sentence.

'Yes, found,' I said.

'Who is he?' he asked.

'You! Who else!'

Amitabh staggered, held the edge of the table. 'What do I have to do?'

'Sign a contract. I assume you can read?' He told me he had graduated from Delhi University. He had performed in many college plays. To this, he added that he had been employed in a major Calcutta firm at Rs 1400 per month. He had a free car, free flat. The emphasis was on 'had'. 'Until yesterday, not now.'

'Why?' I asked, a deliberately foolish question.

'I resigned.'

'Why?'

'You called, so I came.'

'I called only to see you. No one told me that you were in Calcutta. Had I known, I would have thought a dozen times.' Then I made a mental calculation. 'No train runs so fast. You flew down to Bombay?'

'Yes,' he agreed. 'Ajitabh! Did he not mention this to you? He sent me a telegram, which stated: "Role fixed in *Saat Hindustani*. Have to report day after tomorrow."'

I exclaimed, 'He told you such a big lie! What if I had refused to take you?'

'I would have tried elsewhere! Sunil Dutt Sahib is planning a new film. Perhaps he would have taken me. In any case, I was fed up with the Kolkata job.'

In my heart, I appreciated the courage of this young man who had left a steady job on such a flimsy hope. Hope and self-confidence, a good combination.

I said, 'You can go to my secretary and sign the contract. But first answer a few questions. Name?'

'Amitabh.'

'Can't be only Amitabh. Amitabh what?'

'Bachchan. Amitabh Bachchan.'

Alarm bells. 'Are you related to Dr Bachchan?'

'Yes,' he hesitated, 'he is my father.'

'Then this contract cannot be signed today. He is my old friend. I cannot give you this contract without his permission.'

'So send him a telegram asking him. He will reply by tomorrow. But I have already written to him, telling him everything.'

'I cannot write all this in a telegram. It has to be a detailed letter. I will write to him now and ask for a reply by telegram.

You can go now. If we get his permission, you have nothing to worry about. You can come the next day and sign the contract.'

Amitabh left. On the third day, the telegram came. 'If he is working with you, I am happy.'

Now I had no apprehensions, so I signed on Amitabh for Rs 5000. We then began the rehearsals. All the characters and roles were deliberately scrambled, mixed up. The characters had to act 'out of their natural persona'. Famous Bengali actor Utpal Dutt had to act as a Punjabi and deliver the dialogues accordingly. Malayali actor Madhu had to act as a Bengali and learn Bangla. Jalal had to abandon his dapper suits, wear a Maharashtrian dhoti and let the barber take off his beautiful curly hair. Madhu from Meerut had to speak Hindi in a Tamil accent and Anwar Ali (brother of Mahmood and producer of *Khuddar*) had to speak pure, Sanskritized Hindi.

Amitabh as a Bihari Muslim poet had to sing, not recite Urdu couplets, just like my friend, the poet Majaz, used to do. In two days, I realized that whatever instruction was given to Amitabh became 'set in stone' for him. He was the best student of our 'school'.

The question then was, why were we 'mixing' roles? Why? Because we wanted to show that all Indians were one at heart; just change the name and 'accent' and Bengali becomes Punjabi, and 'UPite' becomes Tamil, and Hindu becomes Muslim.

In just a few days, Amitabh became quite fluent in Urdu. In his baritone, he recited so well that the others burst into 'Wah! Wah!' Later, in the film *Kalia* (1981), he recited Urdu with such finesse and perfection. I was happy that the work of *Saat Hindustani* was continuing to bear fruit.

The day we left Dadar Station was memorable. (In 1967 third class was called third class, not the later euphemistic title second class.) Amitabh's coolie came panting, a heavy suitcase on his head. I asked, 'Where is your bedding?'

'In this?' he answered, pointing to the trunk.

The trunk contained his bedding, clothes, a letter pad and a packet of stamped envelopes. On the letter paper, every night, he wrote in detail a letter to his mother. There was a small clock to teach him punctuality. Packed in the trunk was also Amit's very own *qismat*.

In Goa, we could not even afford a modest, leave alone a posh, hotel. We had rented a dak bungalow. We all slept side by side on the floor in a large hall. There were a few exceptions to this community arrangement—Mr and Mrs Utpal Dutt, because they were the seniormost, and Shehnaz Agha, because she was the only girl. Three beds had been arranged for them in a separate small room. Next to me was my assistant Kamlakar, then Amitabh, then Anwar Ali, who became his good friend, then Jalal Agha, etc.

Kamlakar gave Amit the title 'Lambu'. Many years later, when Amitabh had become a big star, Kamlakar met him at R.K. Studios. 'Hello, Amitabh Sahib,' he said hesitatingly. Amit lifted this five feet three inches man off the ground. 'You forget. What did you call me?' By now Kamlakar was scared, 'I used to call you Lambuji then.'

'Not Lambuji . . . you called me Lambu. You thought I had forgotten. So say it, Lambu.' At last Kamlakar was able to say 'Lambu.' Only then he was let go but not before Amitabh had a cup of tea with his old companion!

Amit's image as the 'angry young man' also started with *Saat Hindustani*. The character, as I had written it, evoked mixed emotions in the other characters—suspicion, discrimination, dislike—all because he was Muslim. The prejudice would become palpable from time to time—while eating, drinking, etc. But in the end, the one who is the most fragile, timid and weakest proves the bravest. The Portuguese police inflict the worst kind of torture on him. In the torture chamber, they hook him with electric wires. The current hits his vitals and he faints. They throw water on his face and begin to interrogate him, 'Who are your accomplices in Goa?' The boy refuses to reveal any names and when the cop continues the interrogation, he spits on his face. More lashes break the flesh, but he still doesn't say a word. A blade then slices the skin off his feet which are tied with a rope. At the end they throw him across the border. 'Now, crawl back to your motherland.' In his best close-up of *Saat Hindustani*, Amitabh speaks the words, 'We Indians don't crawl.' He stands upright on his bleeding feet. With trembling legs but straight and raised head he walks towards India. When he reaches the border, he sees his friends. Then he collapses in the arms of his friend Sharma (Anwar Ali).

In this scene, Amitabh presented the finest example of bravery and valour. The violence and fighting that mark his later films began with this scene from *Saat Hindustani*.

Amitabh never likes to use duplicates for his scenes. He never wants to cause pain to anyone. In *Saat Hindustani*, he didn't want anyone else to do the scene because he knew his performance would be appreciated. There was another scene where he was to hang on a rope from a mountain peak. It was like this: The commandos were rope climbing the steepest mountain. Since Amitabh was at the very end, the rope was tied around his waist, so that if he slipped, he could be saved. Amitabh's foot skid and when the others looked down, there he was, flailing his arms and legs. The rock was at least 1000 metres from the gorge.

I had written the scene and my fight master had found a duplicate. He was dressed in the same uniform and, from a distance, looked like Amitabh. The close-up would be taken separately and spliced. Frankly, the shot wouldn't be effective unless it was shot with Amitabh himself. I left the decision to him. 'The duplicate is arranged,' I told him. 'He can be used for the shot.'

'Why? I am not so timid. The rope is strong, isn't it? Then I will do it myself.' Those who saw the shot told me, 'We were terrified—if the rope snapped or slipped what would become of Amitabh.'

This was exactly the emotion we wanted to evoke. One Muslim hangs at the end of a rope. The other end is in the hands of six Hindus. He can be saved only if they all pull together. Will they save him or will they let go and send him to his death? At the end, they all pull together and Amit comes out of the jaws of death.

Since that moment, it seemed Amit began to enjoy this game of brinksmanship. In his later films, he got hurt many times but insisted on doing his own scenes. But, eventually, a near-fatal accident occurred. It was during a scene that had to be done by a duplicate. But Amit put himself at risk and did it himself. The only difference was that the sharp end of the iron table pierced his stomach and he collapsed. What everyone feared had at last come to pass.

The press went wild. Reporters made their spins. Some wrote that it was a blow in his stomach, a flying kick in his stomach, a plot to kill him. The reality was only one: the superstar wanted to personally perform the tableau of life and death.

Amitabh's life hung in balance for two months. Several times rumours of death hit the news. Crores of well-wishers prayed, the best doctors attended to him and nurses worked round the clock. His wife, his brother, his parents did not give up. Prime Minister Indira Gandhi arrived from Delhi to see him.

It was a struggle between life and death. Medicines were flown in from all over the world; many relatives and friends donated blood. This included the wife of the stuntman Puneet Issar whose 'fake blow' was rumoured to be the culprit.

But Amitabh never gave up. Finally, he vanquished death, proving himself the one and only superstar. When a breathing tube was inserted in his neck, he communicated by writing. When Mrs Gandhi visited him, he thanked her with a handwritten note. The prime minister was his mother's oldest friend and he was as dear to her as her own son.

Everything counted. Treatment, surgeries, nursing care, supplications from loving hearts, prayers and pills. Most of all, what mattered was Amitabh's own determination. The hour of death was postponed.

After going through all this, I feel Amitabh does not need to court danger . . . he will have to change his acting style. Kick and kill should be left to younger actors. That does not mean he should quit playing hero (although he has enough wealth to last his whole life).

There are two kinds of courage and two kinds of courageous heroes. One is physical courage, displayed in fight sequences, and the other is spiritual courage. Amitabh Bachchan should now show the courage that he displayed in *Saat Hindustani*. Hanging by the rope against a sheer drop is also courage and walking on sliced feet is also courage. One is life threatening, the other is probably not. What I want to say is that Amitabh has suffered enough physically; he should never risk his life again.

As I was completing this article. Amitabh Bachchan's driver brought me his handwritten letter. It was in response to what I had written about him in *Blitz*.

Breach Candy Hospital
ICU Room # 1
Very dear Mamoojan

I was very moved by your article in *Blitz*. Your appreciation and praise filled me with such courage that I had to fight my illness. With God's grace and your prayers and wishes, I am recovering fast.

I have started walking; soon I will return home. Thank you for your love and kind thoughts.

Amitabh

Sahir Ludhianvi: The Lover and the Beloved

Sir Syed Ahmed Khan was the founder of Aligarh Muslim University and the harbinger of many landmark events. He had once said, 'If Allah asks me, Syed! What did you achieve in this world, my answer will be, "Allah Taa'ala, I got Khwaja Altaf Husain Hali to write his epic poem Musaddas-e-Hali."'

In a similar vein, one of my writings that had the same import was an open letter I wrote to Sahir Ludhianvi in 1948. Sahir was among others who had left for Pakistan. Although this open letter was addressed to Sahir Sahib, I was calling out to all the progressive writers who had performed Hijr'at to Pakistan in the aftermath of the communal riots.

Three months later, I was amazed when I saw Sahir in Bombay. I did not know him well but I admired his poetry, in particular the poem 'Taj Mahal'. The open letter was triggered by that.

'But you had gone away to Pakistan.'

'I had . . . but you called me back.'

He told me that when he read my letter in the newspaper, he was in a dilemma—fifty-fifty in favour of returning to India or staying in Pakistan. My open letter tilted the balance in favour of India. So, he came to India and never went back to Pakistan—although there was no scarcity of admirers and lovers of his poetry in that country.

In a sense then, the responsibility of calling Sahir to India rested on my shoulders.

Inder Raj Anand introduced him to Kardar Sahib and Dr Mahesh Kaul for writing the lyrics for his film *Naujawan* (1951). So, in his very first film, Sahir created history by introducing Urdu poetry in Hindi cinema. From that moment until his dying day, he never deviated from this track. Whatever he wrote was the artistic expression of a poet. He never allowed any dilution in this standard.

He became immensely popular. This was largely due to the beauty of his language and its power of evoking sensitive expression and imagination. He was at once a lover and beloved of Urdu. Lover because he adored the language and got several of his films certified as 'Urdu' by the censor board. He was prepared to suffer, fight and sacrifice for the language. And beloved because Urdu gave him a licence that it had not given to any other poet.

In Urdu poetry, no one has experimented as much as Sahir. He wrote about all of life's faces: political, romantic, psychological. Poetry of the working class, of resistance, poetry of first love, poetry which touched the heights of spiritualism and poetry which was purely tantalizing—all these facets are seen in his film songs.

Sahir was the first to give filmi poetry the status of literature; other poets followed his lead. He not only improved the taste of filmgoers but, like a true poet, never looked down upon the calibre of his audience. Else how could songs like 'Mein pal do pal ka shayar hoon' and 'Ke jaise tujhko banaye gaya hai mere liye' have become as popular as they did!

Sahir means *jadugar* (magician). When Abdul Hai of Ludhiana adopted the *takhallus* 'Sahir' he created magic. Sahiri and Shayiri became synonymous. They were two sides of the same person. I have watched how Sahir's magic grips his listeners. Twenty years ago, we went on a tour to Bihar and western UP under the leadership of Sajjad Zaheer. In Allahabad, at the Kanya Vidyalaya, all the girls were Hindi-speaking. We thought they may not appreciate Urdu poetry. We asked Sahir to recite first. Sahir did not recite elementary-level poetry but presented the best sample of Urdu poetry. The audience was stunned. There was a unanimous request for him to recite his 'Taj Mahal'. Sahir began with the line 'Meri mehboob kahin aur mila kar mujhse' (My beloved, meet me somewhere else). Then he reached the last line, 'Ek shehanshah ne daulat ka sahara lekar, Hum ghareebon ki mohabbat ka uraya hai mazaaq' (An emperor using his boundless wealth made mockery of our love, we the poor). The hall resounded with applause. That day, I said to myself that Sahir's poetry had reached its pinnacle of Sahiri (magic).

Sahir was obsessed with one idea. He wanted to elevate the status of poets within the commercial world of Bombay cinema. No matter how big a film poet was, his name never appeared in the publicity and marketing material. His name was never announced when his songs were played on the radio. He never got decent money for his work; sometimes he got nothing at all! Sahir observed that while music directors and singers were mentioned and applauded, there was no mention of the writer. People knew nothing about poets who had written the words. Sahir considered this attitude to be an insult to the artists. When he was elected vice president of the Film Writers Association (I was president), he accepted the offer on one condition—that the two of us would campaign together for the rights of the poets. We began with the radio. Sahir and I went to Delhi to meet the director general (DG) of All India Radio. We asked, 'You announce the singer's name with every song you play, why do you ignore the poet?' The DG replied, 'We don't have enough time.' Sahir retorted, 'What about the time spent announcing the names of those who send requests?' The DG was finally convinced, and an order was issued that the name of the poet would be announced with every song.

As recognition of this achievement, Sahir was elected president of Film Writers' Association. Sahir kept up his struggle against the government and film producers for film writers and poets. By now, Sahir's popularity had reached a point where he could ask anything for himself, whether on radio or film. But Sahir was more socially conscious; he never thought of personal success, he wanted collective good—his was the Marxian struggle. He wanted rights for what he called 'brain labour'. Until all 'brains' were guaranteed rights, he was not willing to give up his struggle.

He was humane; he loved and respected his fellow beings. Within him he had all human weaknesses and all the strengths.

A friend to the last—that was what Sahir was! Once, when I broke my ribs in a cab accident, Sahir took me in his car for an X-ray. It was discovered that I had broken four ribs. I was placed in a cast. This man stood by me all through. He just didn't take me to the hospital in his car, he: *'Dost aan bashad ke gir-e-dast o dost. Dar pareshaaan haali–o-darmandagi'* (A friend is one who holds the hand of a friend, when he is miserable or dejected). Many friends can narrate such incidents about Sahir.

We travelled almost 2000 miles in Bihar and UP in Sahir's car. Not even once did he make us feel that the car and petrol were his and we were free riders at his expense.

I had one complaint. Whenever he invited us for dinner, he first fed all his guests and always ate last. Once I got so angry that I left his home without having dinner.

He came to my house the next day, a little before lunch. 'You left last night without having dinner,' he complained.

'That is true. But we came to eat with you. But you were not at the table, so what was the point of eating?'

'What you did was fine. But I didn't eat last night.'

'Why?'

'How could I? When my dear friend went home hungry, how could I eat? The idea was to eat together. If not at mine, then we can do it in your house.'

'Meaning?'

'Meaning, I have come to eat with you. Without notice. May I?'

'Sure, I would be delighted.'

Food was laid out on the table.

We both ate the humble food with relish.

'Last night, at your house, there were two types of pulao, one biryani. There were also shami kebabs, murgh musallam and two types of dessert. Today there is only boiled cauliflower and masur dal.'

'That was all for show. Last night, I did not want people to say that a poet didn't serve them a decent meal. What is placed before us today is real food.'

He had three rotis, cauliflower and dal.

I had three rotis.

Then we washed our hands.

While parted he said, 'Thank you very much.'

'Why are you embarrassing me?'

'I came here to erase my embarrassment.'

'Now I am embarrassed. I could not give you dessert.'

'Well . . . you owe me dessert,' saying this, Sahir left.

I used to think of Sahir as my junior by several years. After his death, I found out he was fifty-nine years old. I was seven years older than him. Then why did he look so young?

That is because, besides being good looking, he dressed well, spoke well and was well disposed. He always dressed in spotless white, his car was also white—no dirt visible anywhere. He always spoke to me with the utmost respect. So, I like felt a *buzurg* in his presence.

My heart aches when I write 'was' against his name; he was always 'is' in my life. They said three things about him: first, matchless poet, second, most published poet, third, maintained high standard of poetry and exalted the status of poets in film hierarchy.

He used to say, 'I won't write for big music directors and singers.' This was not a personal whim; it was his confidence in his own creative ability. He loved working with non-commercial, small music directors. Sahir never had a problem with changing a word or line if asked by the music or film director. But he could not tolerate being bullied by commercial lure.

Air travel was anathema for him. He travelled thousands of miles by car, but despised taking flights. There must have been deep-seated fear. I wanted to ask him about it but death intervened before I could. He drove his car and never expressed any apprehension of a road mishap.

He came to visit me three days before he died. We sat together; there was no visible sign of illness or weakness. We spoke of literature. A publisher had asked him to publish his works in English. I had translated two or three of his long poems. Despite my prosaic style, he had liked my work. He wanted me to translate more—both his ghazals and *nazms*. I agreed. But he was not satisfied. 'I have called the publisher here so we can have a face-to-face meeting. You will do this work for my sake, but why should a trader take advantage of our personal friendship? Suppose I were to die? I don't want anyone to take unethical advantage so face-to-face is the only way.'

I laughed off his apprehension. 'Sahir Sahib, I am many years ahead of you in the queue. The question does not arise.'

He laughed. 'Abbas Sahib, the question may not arise, but people are suddenly summoned up there!' He pointed towards the sky.

Forty-eight hours later, in the middle of the night, the phone rang. The voice at the other end asked, 'Is it true that Sahir Sahib is dead?'

'What nonsense. He is fine. People love to spread falsehoods.' I gave this person his phone number, which I always remembered because it was similar to mine. 'Why don't you call this number and find out?' I told the stranger as I banged down the phone.

Ten minutes later he called again. 'I called many times. There is no answer.' I snapped back, 'So that is enough proof that his phone is out of order, and they all are asleep. Good night.'

Half an hour later, a good friend called from Sahir's house. 'We have just brought Sahir Sahib from Dr Kapoor's Versova home. *Inna hillah-e-we inna allaihe raja'oon.*'

It was then that it dawned on me. Sahir, who was called 'Naujawan' because the first film for which he wrote was *Naujawan* (1951), who looked every bit a *naujawan,* had broken the queue, leaving us oldies far behind.

Rajinder Singh Bedi: The Guru

His very first short-story collection, *Dana o Daam* (1939), created a sensation. It won an award from Punjab government. My brother Khwaja Ghulamus Saiyidain introduced his work to me with the words, 'Remember that name; one day he will be a great writer.' In those days, very few people knew Bedi. Lucknow critics ignored him, saying 'How can Punjabis write in Urdu?' But it is equally true that Punjabi, more than any other language, can be credited with the greatest role in the development of Urdu.

My initiation into Urdu literature was through Bedi Sahib's writings, hence for me he is unforgettable. I invited him to Bombay when I met him in Lahore. But things changed very quickly and, instead of Bombay, our next meeting was in Srinagar (for the Progressive Writers Association meet). Bedi Sahib was staying in guest house number four with the other writers. I was with the journalists in another guest house. But in the evenings, I hung out with Bedi and the other writers. I enjoyed his effervescent *'baagh o bahar'* personality. He spoke

as fluently as his pen moved. That was 1948; Kashmir became
the theatre of the worst tribal onslaught. That moment was
historical. Every day the Kashmir National Conference's
urban volunteers combated with tribal intruders. Conditions
were fragile. But progressive writers, who had come from
different corners of the country—most of whom considered
Bedi Sahib as their guru—met every evening in his room and
read out their latest writings.

I too felt like reading something but I had not written much
except a story titled 'Ababeel', which in any case was not with
me. So, one day, I shut myself in my room and began writing
about an experience of my family. It concerned an elderly Sikh
gentleman who saved the life of his Muslim neighbour and, in
the bloodbath, lost his own life. The impact of this supreme
sacrifice changed the life of the Muslim family, who gave up
their prejudices. At the end, the communal Muslim, who is the
narrator, says these words, 'It was not Sardarji who was dying; it
was I who was slowly dying . . . the old I!' That night I finished
the story and went to the guest house where the session was just
concluding. 'I have brought my brand-new story,' I announced.
'Let us hear it,' they all said. I pointed at Bedi Sahib and said,
'It may be offensive to you but it is not me who is speaking; it
is a communal Muslim. So let me beg forgiveness beforehand.'

There were fifteen to twenty people in the room. Most
of them were progressive writers from Delhi and Allahabad,
two of them were Sikh writers and a couple were Sikh *sipahis*.
I began reading. Every now and then I looked at Bedi Sahib to
note his changing expressions. 'Why are you looking at me?' he
asked. 'Because of all present, you are the most senior sardar,'
I replied. When I read the climax of the story, I noticed tears
in Bedi Sahib's eyes. He embraced me. 'You have written a

fine story. Send it to *Adab-e-Lateef* so that Pakistanis know that such sardarjis live in India.' He added, 'It is an excellent story but beware of my community. They should not harm you. My people are really quite stupid.'

On Bedi Sahib's suggestion, I sent my story to *Adab-e-Lateef* and forgot about it. Eight months later, I returned to Kashmir. Pandit Jawaharlal Nehru had sent me to counter the anti-India propaganda that was being broadcast on Pakistani radio every day. Bedi Sahib was in Jammu, where he had taken charge of Jammu Radio.

Next, he moved to All India Radio, where there was a unique literary collective with renowned personalities like Saadat Hasan Manto, Faiz Ahmed Faiz, N.M. Rashid, Upendra Nath Ashk and Krishan Chander. Bedi started writing radio features and plays, and soon became known all over India. His writings had everything: theme, content and language. From there he entered the film world, where he soon grew in stature because of his ability to write scripts in both languages, Urdu and Punjabi.

His first associate was the Punjabi director D.D. Kashyap, who was making films in partnership with Baburao Pai. Before that he had worked with Shantaram in Pune's Prabhat Film Company. Bedi's first assignment was to write the screenplay and dialogue for *Badi Behan* (1949). Rajinder Singh Bedi shot to fame soon after its release.

Those days, he lived in Matunga. Once or twice a week, either I visited him or he came to me in Juhu. Or we met at Krishan Chander's house. Over time I came to know him closely.

His next film was *Daag* (1952), directed by Amiya Chakravarty, in which Dilip Kumar and Nimmi played the lead roles. *Daag* (1952) was an unconventional film in which

Bedi Sahib's dialogues were off the beaten track. The film proved to be a big hit. Now he was at the top of that ilk. When the film *Mirza Ghalib* (1954) got the President's Gold Medal, his fame reached new heights. So, when Bimal Roy decided to remake *Devdas* (1955), he gave the responsibility for the dialogues to Bedi.

If Bimal Roy gets the credit for making a successful film out of the Bengali classic novel and Dilip Sahib for playing Devdas in his unique style, Bedi gets the credit for giving it a new life with his superb dialogues. Another joint effort of Bedi and Dilip Kumar was *Madhumati* (1958), which was essentially a romantic story, but Bedi ensured its high literary quality.

I was now regularly seeing him every week.

In those days, my house was a meeting point for progressive writers. By now, several of Bedi Sahib's collections had been published. One collection of his radio plays was called *Bejaan Cheezein* (Lifeless Things), and a classic long-short story or novelette was titled *Ek Chadar Maili Si*. He first read the story in my house; we were all stunned. No one spoke for a few minutes. Then there was thunderous applause which made my neighbours rush in to ask if all was well. That day I made a passionate statement. I said that this short novel was of the calibre of Hemingway's *Old Man and the Sea*. It also deserved a Nobel Prize. Others agreed with me but the argument that evening was whether it should be called a long-short story or a short novel.

Geeta Bali loved this literary piece and wanted to make a film in which she would perform the title role. She began working on it, but her sudden, tragic death put an end to that. Then a Pakistani actress, Sangeeta, made a good film based on Bedi's story.

Bedi Sahib wrote a script based on his radio story 'Naql Makani' and with it entered the film industry as producer-director. He made the film Dastak (1970) which was a commercial success but was considered both experimental and a 'shocker'. His direction resulted in excellent performances by Sanjeev Kumar and Rehana Sultan; they both received the National Award for best actor and actress. Madan Mohan got the best music director for his excellent work. Dastak made Bedi Sahib join the short line-up of sensitive and accomplished directors. People had even higher expectations from him. The government awarded him the Padma Shri for his outstanding work.

He then made a commercial film, Phagun (1973), which failed both on the commercial and artistic front—'Na Khuda hi mila na visaal e sanam'. He suffered big losses and for several years could not think of making a film.

After many years he began making a film, Ankhein Dekhi (1978), which was about atrocities against Dalits. He took a new girl and boy in lead roles and made it in his very own way. Unfortunately, the film could not be released.

In Bombay, Bedi Sahib was well known for his cheerful, easy-going temperament. Despite spending thirty years in the industry, he never allowed himself to be immersed in the colours of Bombay.

He had become very despondent since the tragic death of his wife and son. Fate then played a cruel game, and he became paralysed. When I visited him in the hospital, his words filled my eyes with tears. He had an indomitable will which enabled him to bear all this and stay alive. His biggest pain was that he could not use his pen again. This pain stayed with him until the end. With this pain in his heart, he left the world.

A writer's death is a double tragedy. His own death and the death of creativity. If only there had been more time.

All of us are thus doubly afflicted.

Satyajit Ray: Mahapurush

When I first met Satyajit Ray he was not a famous film-maker, but I had been hearing about him from friends. Everyone was talking about him in the artistic circles of Calcutta—a man who was making art films for which he would shoot only on Sundays. This was because, at the time, he was a full-time art director in a well-known advertising company; he was also involved in the Indian People's Theatre Association, of which I was general secretary.

I phoned the ad company where he worked and took an appointment. I had to climb three floors to reach his office. He came outside his small office the minute he was handed my card. Our first meeting was on the staircase leading to his office floor. There, he and I stood and talked for a long time, leaning against the wall. The first thing I noticed was his height; I had never seen a person who was six feet four inches tall. For a small man like me it was difficult to talk because I had to crane my neck just to look at him.

One thing led to another. I found out that not only physically but in several other ways he was very lofty, especially his mind. Very soon I found myself under the spell of his persona. At the time, I had completed my film *Dharti ke Lal* (1946). He had seen it several times and told me that he liked it a lot. He also said that this film made him realize that in India we could make natural and realistic films using amateur actors. At the time I was writing *Awara* (1956) for Raj Kapoor and also making my own film, *Anhonee* (1973). Despite my multifaceted work, I realized that Satyajit Ray knew much more about films than I did, especially about European cinema of which he had deep knowledge. More than American cinema, he was impressed with Italian and French.

In Bombay theatres, most European films were not even shown. I asked him where he had seen these films. He told me that he had seen several during his short stay in London and the rest at the Calcutta Film Society.

We began talking about film societies; I had to admit that even in this respect Calcutta had outdone us. In Bombay there was nothing called Film Society; I decided that this had to be rectified.

After that, I heard from friends that he was making his own film but under so much financial constraint that he had to pawn his wife's jewellery. He shot his film only on a Sunday or a holiday. I also learnt that the Bengal chief minister heard about Ray's incomplete film, so he got the Community Development Ministry to sanction a loan. When the film *Pather Panchali* (1955) was finally released, it became a big hit and received the President of India's gold medal. At the awards ceremony, people noticed that the gold medal was strung around the neck of a government official. Two or three years passed; we in Bombay could not see the film but the Calcutta newspapers reported that the magic of Bengal was working in the film world. *Pather Panchali* was a stunning piece.

In 1955 I went to London with my film *Munna* (1954), which was to be presented at the Edinburgh Festival. By that time *Pather Panchali* had received international fame and awards at various festivals.

Munna received good reviews at the Edinburgh Festival and some English critics wrote about it. Based on these, the British Film Institute decided to show it at their theatre. It was good fortune that along with *Pather Panchali* it was considered a fine example of Indian cinema. *Pather Panchali* was shown for four days and *Munna* for three in the week-long programme.

Ray's films began to be produced every year. First, he completed the Apu series. After the child grows up, he sees his father dying in Benaras. In this film, Satyajit Ray used a remarkable cinematographic metaphor: as the father takes his last breath, a band of pigeons sitting in a tree suddenly rises and gets lost in the sky. It was as if the dead man's spirit rises up and dissolves in the same sky.

The third in this series was the film *Apur Sansar* (1959). The boy has now grown up and steps into the life of a newly married man. The marital relationship is shown with such sensitivity and honesty that its parallel has not been seen in Indian cinema. For the audience, however, this film became known for Sharmila Tagore's debut. Sharmila in *Apur Sansar* is an innocent face, untouched by Bombay studios' trademark paint and powder. Today she has moved far away from that persona. Before the third film of the series, Satyajit made a comedy called *Parash Pathar* (1958), a satire on our society, but this film was a box office flop. People who knew Satyajit Ray expected art films from him, not satire. In any case, in our country, there is very little understanding of satire as a literary genre.

Among all of Satyajit's films, the best after *Pather Panchali* is *Debi* (1960). The 'old' Sharmila Tagore's excellent acting, besides the chiaroscuro, the turn and twist of the story is so remarkable that one cannot take one's eyes off the screen. It reminds one of Eisenstein's *Ivan the Terrible* (1944).

In *Jalsaghar* (1958), Satyajit shows the decline of the zamindari system; the film is also his last word on the system. His subsequent films are about the Bengali middle class.

Nayak (1966) portrays a progressive playwright who narrates the story of his life. Some people think Ray is hereby showing his own life but I have a different view. It is a warning by this sensitive artist, a warning to himself, that if he compromises with the business class, then his art will be doomed. His artistic values will be drowned in the storm of currency, the kind of storm that is repeatedly shown in the film as a dream sequence.

In *Mahanagar* (1963), *Pratidwandi* (1970) and *Aranyer Din Ratri* (1970) you see the youth of Calcutta who work in offices, youth who look for jobs, youth who are unemployed, who dream of becoming officers, working girls—every character is alive, real. The artist has used soft undertones for these artists, never stark black-and-white contrast. There is, however, one weakness in his films, if I can call it that. Ray shows people speaking only in Bengali with a few English words thrown in. But Calcutta is a metropolis; besides Bengali you also hear Punjabi, Tamil and Telugu. However, there is no trace in his films of anyone speaking these languages. I feel that the use of different languages would have given yet another dimension to his film. The fact is that Ray is not comfortable using any language other than Bengali or English. As an artist he is a perfectionist; that is why he does not use a language over which he does not have full command.

Besides these films he made some children's films too. *Goopi Gyne Bagha Byne* (1969) is clearly a fantasy, but within its childlike layers it carries the message of world peace. His second film, *Sonar Kella* (1974), is about a child who vaguely remembers his previous incarnation. Some greedy people smell a hidden treasure and follow the child to an ancient castle in Rajasthan in the hope that he will lead them to a buried fortune. The child spots a dancing peacock and begins to run towards him. The story ends right there; you can derive whatever meaning you want. I came away with the feeling that Satyajit Ray wanted to show that life's not about a gold casket, a buried treasure or a peacock crafted in gold. For an innocent child (or artist), life is nature in all her glory; a peacock dancing in a wooded clearing.

Satyajit Ray is not only an excellent director, he is also a very good artist. He has illustrated many children's books as well as posters for his own films. For every scene he makes a sketch, thereby creating a unique album. His art does not stop here. Besides directing and painting, he plays beautiful melodies on his grand piano. His love for music is reflected in his friendships with maestros like Ravi Shankar and Vilayat Khan. They all have scored music for some of his films. But now he directs the music himself.

People consider documentary film-making a special art; the few documentaries made by Ray are unique examples of this genre. There is one called *Inner Eye* (1972) which is about a blind artist and professor in Shantiniketan; I consider it his best. Ten years ago, he made a very good one on Tagore; not surprising because he was trained at Shantiniketan, and Tagore had a deep influence over him. Those who say that his

art is greatly influenced by French director Renoir and other
European directors forget one thing. The roots of every person
and especially of every artist have to be sought in his own earth.
I feel that his initial inspiration springs from his own land and
surroundings. The artist who has left the deepest impression
on him is Tagore. Next is Nitin Bose who is a close relative,
and must have been inspirational for his nephew. As a child, he
must have seen the films of Debaki Bose and Barua. It wouldn't
be surprising if the old art films of Shantaram also left a deep
impact on his subconscious mind.

I am not one of those people who think that Satyajit Ray's
birth was a miracle, that before him there was no Indian cinema
and after him Indian cinema will cease to exist. I don't consider
this vacuum as a sign of an artist's greatness. Ray is a great film
director but he is not apart from the Indian tradition; he is a
gem embedded in the ring of Indian art.

Besides being a big artist, Satyajit Ray has weaknesses and
strengths as other human beings. He was a rebel son who left
his family tradition and carved his own path. But he has great
respect for his father from whom he inherited literature and
art. He is also a loving father to his only son; I am sure his son
Sandeep will turn out to be a rebel like him and discover new
trends in film direction. His wife is herself a great artist of the
IPTA group. But she sacrificed her art to help his. They love
each other but also fight as all loving couples do. Satyajit Ray
does not drink; he smokes the best cigarettes. He used to live
in a small flat which was too small for his piano, his books and
his gramophone records. Now he lives in a spacious flat which
is enough for all his needs. He sits on an armchair and writes
as he sips his tea. He is often seen in a simple pair of pants and

shirt, sometimes kurta pyjama; on special occasions he wears a dhoti and kurta.

He wants art to be appreciated, whether his own or of others. When my film *Shehar Aur Sapna* (1963) was stalled for lack of money, I showed four reels of the incomplete film to him. He liked it very much and said to me, 'Why do you worry, a little bit of money is all you need.' After its completion he watched the film and wrote some words of appreciation. He had no regret when instead of his *Mahanagar, Shehar Aur Sapna* won the President's Gold Medal for best film.

The high point of his career was when the British Federation of Film Societies, in its golden jubilee celebration, declared him as the most outstanding film director.

Now Satyajit's career faces the biggest challenge—his first Hindustani film *Shatranj Ke Khiladi* (1977) in which he has cast Sanjeev Kumar. For him, our Hindustani film world is a strange one. I don't know whether he will be able to do justice to the Premchand story in Hindustani language. But in a way the success of Shyam Benegal's *Ankur* (1974) and *Nishant* (1975) has opened the way for him. At the same time, these two films have given an artistic challenge to Ray's first Hindi language film. If this film is successful both commercially and artistically then it will be a golden day in the history of Indian cinema.

I remember Delhi Film Festival, 1955; on the last day, photographers were taking shots of jury members. They made me stand next to Ray. It was as if Sri Lanka was dangling beneath India! I said to him, I am so embarrassed standing next to you. He replied, do you think I am less embarrassed!

Sometimes being tall also becomes an awkward proposition!

KAHAANIYAAN

As a writer, Khwaja Ahmad Abbas consciously depicted the tales of ordinary people. His concerns for the man on the street as well as his humanism drew his vision and thought to those on the margins, trying to navigate their way through life and circumstances.

The second section of this book is a series of short stories based around the world of films. Drawn from his own experiences, stories such as 'A Mother's Heart', 'Kayakalp' and 'The Filmi Triangle' take us behind the scenes to the competitive, harsh, often rapacious world of films that is seldom seen or talked about. In 'Actress', Abbas turns his critical eye upon himself, admonishing his hasty judgement and learning an invaluable lesson in the bargain. A thinly veiled reference to Meena Kumari, the heartbreaking 'Parineeta Kumari's Paans' is a look at the star's last days, as well as the profound effect she had on those around her.

Gender is an integral theme in these stories, wherein we observe the tenuous status of women in the film industry. Subject to impossible standards of beauty and youth, they bear the brunt of the brickbats as glamorous icons yet their marginalized position is made evident in the male-dominated world of films.

A Mother's Heart

The studio was bustling with activity. The hairdresser was fixing a wig on the hero's head. The heroine was examining her lipstick in the mirror. The director turned his attention from the dialogue writer to the cameraman. In one corner, the production manager was fixing his commission with the person who supplied extras.

The cameraman's assistants looked at the lights through the camera lens and announced, 'The shot is ready!'

The cameraman surveyed the scene himself and then shouted to the director, 'The shot is ready.'

The director went up to the hero and softly said, 'The shot is ready.'

The hero sucked on his cigarette contentedly, examined his head carefully from the front to the back in the two mirrors, adjusted his wig, patted down a strand of artificial hair and stood up. He looked in the direction of the assistant director who was standing with the dialogue file and asked, 'What film is this?'

'*A Mother's Heart.*'

'What scene is it?'

'The one with the child.'

'With the child! But I am not married in this film, so how can there be a child?'

'No, this is not your child. You find an orphan on the streets and, on seeing him, you are reminded of your own childhood and your mother. You take the child in your arms, and you are overcome with emotion. With tears in your eyes, you say . . . '

'Yes, okay, so tell me the dialogue,' saying this, the hero sat back down on the chair.

The dialogue director immediately opened the file and started reading. 'This child is also the *noor* of someone's eye . . . '

'Noor? What is noor?' the hero asked.

The dialogue director scratched his bald head with his pencil quizzically, 'Umm . . . noor is just noor . . . like Muhammed Noorul Hassan, etc. Actually, the writer has used this word to give the dialogue rhythm.'

'Read the entire dialogue.'

'This child is also the noor of someone's eyes, the *suroor* of someone's heart. If this child is hungry and *majboor*, it is the *kusoor* of society. This child can grow up and become a doctor, lawyer or a prominent leader . . . '

'What is this nonsense?' said the hero, looking at the director. 'I won't be able to remember such a long dialogue.'

'Yes, this dialogue is unnecessarily long,' the director agreed. He instructed the dialogue director, 'Do as Mr Kumar says. Shorten the dialogue.'

The dialogue director made a huge cross on the page with his blue-coloured pencil and said, 'Mr Kumar, you tell me.'

The hero thought for a moment. 'Write this: This child is also his mother's heart.'

'And after that?'

'That's all, nothing more. This child is also his mother's heart.'

The dialogue director repeated the words, 'This child is also his mother's heart. Bravo! What a dialogue! Mr Kumar, you should have been a writer.'

He turned towards the director and said, 'Sir, this is the theme dialogue of the film.'

'So, let's go, the shot is ready.' The director beckoned the hero and as the hero got off his chair, everyone else followed suit.

'Bring the child,' the assistant director's voice boomed.

'Bring the child,' shouted the second assistant director.

'Bring the child,' called the third assistant director.

'Supplier!' commanded the production manager, 'where is the child?'

'Mrs Johnson,' shouted the extras supplier.

A large, middle-aged Anglo-Indian woman emerged carrying a child with brown eyes and round face, wearing a nylon frock.

'This frock looks too fine. How can this belong to a poor child?' the third assistant protested. 'Just see how much realism there is in the films of Satyajit Ray.'

'Dressman,' shouted the second assistant.

'Yes, Sir,' the dressman replied.

'Change the child's frock. Make him wear a dirty, torn piece of clothing,' the first assistant commanded.

The dressman fished around in a box, brought out a handful of dirty shreds and walked towards the child.

The child's mother saw the rags and immediately clutched the child to her chest, 'No, no, my baby will not wear these dirty clothes. What if he catches some infection?'

'But Memsahib, this is important for realism,' the third assistant started to explain.

She interrupted him saying, 'My baby only works in high-class movies. I told the supplier that my baby will not wear dirty clothes.'

The director gestured towards his assistant, 'Let it be. These days even the children of poor parents wear nylon clothes.'

The hero was standing in front of the camera. He extended his arms towards the mother saying, 'Come on, baby.'

The child quickly leapt into the hero's arms. Everyone heaved a sigh of relief. It is believed that during a shoot, three problems can make your life miserable—a horse, a dog and a child!

The child's mother flicked her thick brown hair, stared deeply into the hero's eyes and said, 'My baby is sweet, isn't he? He will also grow up to become a hero in the movies.'

The cameraman moved the camera slightly from the left to the right and then moved it back again, to the same spot. He peered into the eye of the camera and said, 'Mr Kumar, please come a little forward . . . that's it, that's it . . . perfect.' He then shouted out, 'Ready for sound test.'

The sound assistant brought the microphone forward. 'Mr Kumar, please say the dialogue once.'

The hero looked at the microphone lovingly and said, 'This child is also his mother's heart.'

'Howzat?' the three assistants shouted in unison as if this were a cricket match and they were fielders turning expectantly to the umpire, awaiting a leg before wicket verdict.

The response came through a loudspeaker in the sound room, 'Okay, ready for the take.'

The first assistant director shouted, 'Silence'.

The second assistant director shouted, 'Silence.'

The third assistant director shouted, 'No talking.'

The director said, 'Sound start.'

A response came from the sound room, 'Camera.'

The cameraman pushed a button and said, 'Running.'

The hero picked up the child in his arms once again, looked at the camera passionately and said, 'This child is also . . . ' He had just said this much when the child grabbed a lock of hair on the hero's forehead, pulling the wig off!

The hero's bald head shone bright as day under the harsh studio lights.

The director nervously shouted, 'Cut! Cut!'

The first assistant director shouted, 'Cut it.'

The second assistant director shouted, 'Cut it.'

The third assistant director called out, 'Make-up, call the hairdresser.'

Three young college girls who were ardent fans of Kumar had especially come to watch the shooting. They reeled under the shock that the object of their adoration was absolutely bald and his scalp as white as an egg!

'Oh god!' exclaimed one to the other. 'He is bald!'

The other said, 'Shh, speak softly. He'll hear you.'

Kumar stomped off angrily, and his hairdresser attempted to fit his wig once again in his make-up room.

'This time, I'll put in four hairclips so that the wig won't come off even if it is pulled.'

'I will not work with this child,' Kumar replied in a fury.

When the hero emerged after securing the wig on his head, he heard the director tell the child's mother, 'Sorry, Memsahib, but that's it for today. We'll certainly try to find a role for him in some other scene.'

'That's all right,' said the memsahib. 'I am aware that such things happen during shootings. Tell your manager to settle our account.'

The production manager handed over Rs 60 to the extras supplier and took a receipt for Rs 75. The supplier gave Rs 40 to the woman and took a receipt of Rs 55. The memsahib was just about to sit in a taxi with the child when he grabbed her hair and yanked her wig off as well! The mother quickly patted her artificial hair back on to her head, glancing around furtively to see if anybody had noticed. Seeing no one around, she heaved a sigh of relief and cooed, 'You naughty baby.'

She instructed the taxi driver, 'Driver, drop us off at the Dadar station. We will take a train to Byculla from there.'

The studio was once again in a state of upheaval.

The director told his assistant to call for a replacement, 'Arrange for another child.'

The first assistant said to the production manager, 'Bring another child.'

The production manager took the extras supplier to one corner and said, 'You are minting money these days! Bring another child and arrange for one or two others as well. The more kids, the better for us.'

The extras supplier took the producer's car and returned shortly with a chubby boy who seemed to be about three or four years old. Accompanying him was a dark, fat and well-built man with long hair. He was wearing a striped vest and checked lungi.

'We are here, Sir,' said the muscular man to the director with a salute.

'Who are you?'

'Don't you recognize me? I am Master Gutthal. I have been working in the industry for a long time. I worked as a villain in *Prince Ghulfam* and was a side-hero in *Baaghi Shehzaadi*, and a side-villain in *Lal Ghoda*. I still play character roles. What are your instructions for me? I am at your service.'

The director said in irritation, 'Right now, we only require a child.'

'The child is also here, sir,' said the man and pushed the boy forward.

'Say hello to Director Sir.'

The child was wearing a pair of green shorts and a shirt made of velvet. He was holding a small toy in one hand but his face did not seem very childlike. It almost seemed like a middle-aged man had been dwarfed in size. Imitating his father, he too gave a salute and continued to stand in that position till his father gave him the next command.

'Do the twist and show Sir.'

The child, with the unchildlike face, started to do the twist like a wind-up doll.

'Well done, well done,' said the father, clapping and keeping a beat for the dance. The child swayed his hips, moving backwards and forwards, left and right.

Slowly, the people on the set—the cameraman, his assistant, lights men, minor character actors, extras—all stopped to watch the child.

The producer whispered into the director's ear, 'Stop all this. We have to pay Mr Kumar Rs 10, 000 for the day's shoot and we haven't taken a single shot yet.'

The director commanded, 'Cut it.'

The child immediately stopped, like an automaton.

The director ordered the first assistant, 'Call Mr Kumar.'

The first assistant said to the second assistant, 'Tell Mr Kumar that the child is here. The shot is ready.'

The third assistant ran towards the make-up room.

The hero entered the studio and immediately asked, 'Where is the child?'

The boy in the green shorts greeted the hero with a military-style salute, 'Good morning. How do you do?' On saying this, he winked at the hero, catching him off guard. The hero leapt back in surprise. On seeing his reaction, everyone started laughing.

'So, champ, will you work in the film? You won't get scared, will you?'

The child spoke with a child-like stutter and said, 'You will be the one to be afraid.' On hearing this, another burst of laughter went around and the hero asked irritatedly, 'Will I have to put this troublemaker on my lap?'

The cameraman shouted, 'Ready for take.'

Various other voices echoed, 'Ready for take' followed by 'All lights . . . hairdresser . . . sound test . . . '

'Hold on! First let me pick up this little wrestler and see,' said the hero.

He managed to pick the child up. But he was heavy as a rock and the hero was soon out of breath from the exertion.

'Sound start,' the director called out.

'Camera,' answered the sound recordist.

'Running,' declared the cameraman.

The hero looked at the child lovingly, the child winked at him and the hero blurted out, 'This child is also . . . this child is also . . . '

The child said, 'You've forgotten the dialogue, haven't you?'

The hero felt that the boy in his arms was some demon kid and, saying 'Cut it', threw him towards the father. In this way, the muscular man pocketed Rs 60 and walked out of the studio.

A third child was brought in. Just before the shot, he peed on the hero's suit. The hero said, 'I won't work with him.'

A fourth child was brought in. He looked quite innocent and everyone thought that the shot would go as planned. But just as the hero picked him up, he started writhing and wailing at the top of his lungs. He stopped crying only when he was put back in the mother's arms. He remained quiet when he was placed on the hero's lap once again, but as soon as the camera started rolling and the hero said the dialogue, 'This child is also . . . ' he started crying and kicked the hero so hard that he almost took out his eye!

The hero announced his decision, 'I will not work with this child either. Either get me a well-behaved child or cancel the scene. My shift is going to end in an hour's time in any case.'

The supplier said, 'How many children can I keep supplying? At this rate, we will reject all the children in Bombay!'

The production manager said, 'What's your problem? You are minting money . . .'

'And you aren't?' the supplier shot back.

'Yes, yes we both are. Now bring a well-behaved child from somewhere.'

'I have already brought all the film kids I knew. Every mother does not allow her child to work in films. These are the only four people who do business with their kids.'

'Come on, anyone will agree to bring their kids into the business for money.'

The two of them had stepped out of the studio. A woman was sweeping the road there.

'Hold on, one moment,' the production manager called out to her. 'You are spreading dust everywhere. Is this the time to be sweeping the place? Why didn't you do this in the morning?'

'Sir, I got late today.'

'If you came in late, then your pay will get cut. Do you work for free here?'

'Sir,' the woman pleaded, 'My child is unwell.'

'What has happened?'

'Sir, I don't know what has happened, but his fever hasn't broken in the past ten days.'

'So why haven't you taken him to a doctor?'

'I took him to the doctor in our locality, sir, and paid the Rs 2 fee as well.'

'You should take him to a child specialist.'

'Their fee is Rs 25 and it costs extra for the medicines. If I can get my salary early this month, I can get my child treated there.'

'Bring your child. You'll get Rs 40 for the full treatment,' the extra supplier said, winking surreptitiously at the production manager.

The production manager said, 'Your child will be photographed in a film with Mr Kumar and you'll even get paid for it. Quickly go and bring your child.'

'I'll bring him at once, Sir,' said the sweeper, casting away her broom.

'But listen, if the child cries and makes a nuisance, you will not get paid. He should remain quiet.'

The woman lived in a shanty just behind the studio. Before entering her home, she knocked on her neighbour's door.

'What is it, Chawali?' asked the neighbour.

'My child cries a lot and I need to go for work. Please give me that medicine you give your child when you leave for work.'

The neighbour handed her a small pouch, 'Just dissolve a little bit in water.'

The woman went in. The child was lying all alone on the bare mat, crying. She picked him up; his body was burning with fever. Chawali adoringly said to her child, 'Don't cry, my love. Come, I'll take you to a film studio. My son will become the hero of a film. Then I'll take you to a good doctor. Don't cry my love, don't cry.' On saying this, she took a bit of the medicine, dissolved it in water and made him drink the black-coloured liquid. The child's cry reduced to hiccups, and he slowly fell asleep. Chawali wrapped him up in a cloth and started walking towards the studio.

'Will he cry?' asked the extra supplier.

'No, Sir. He is sleeping soundly,' said Chawali.

'Hey, will the child start crying?' asked the director.

'No Sir, he is a very well-mannered child. He has just had his milk and is sleeping contentedly. You can take as many shots as you need,' replied the production manager.

'Will the child start crying?' the hero asked before picking up the child.

'No, Mr. Kumar,' the director assured him. 'They have found a quiet, well-behaved child and brought him.'

The hero placed the child on his lap and thought to himself, 'Thank god this child is not too heavy.' Then he said, 'Quickly take the shot while the child is sleeping peacefully. If he wakes up, he too will become a nuisance.'

'Ready for take.'

'Ready for take.'

'All lights.'

'Sound ready?'

'Start sound.'

'Camera.'

'Running clip.'

'*A Mother's Heart*, scene 25, shot 7, take 4.'

The hero picked up the child and gazed at his face. The child was sleeping peacefully. There was a strange smile on his innocent face. The hero looked at the camera and spoke from the depths of his heart, 'This child is also the heart of a mother.'

The shot was cut, but the cameraman said that he wanted another take as the light on the child's face was not at the right angle.

Once again, the hero said, 'This child is also his mother's heart.'

Just then, an airplane flew above the studio and its sound filtered into the loudspeaker.

'Cut, cut . . . airplane.'

For one reason or the other, the shot was repeated several times and was finally okayed on the ninth take. The hero handed the child over to the production manager. He was still fast asleep.

The production manager gave the child to the extras supplier.

The supplier placed the child on Chawali's lap, handed her Rs 40 and got her thumb impression on a receipt of Rs 55.

'Go, take him to a good doctor now and get a proper treatment.'

'Sir, I will go there right away in a taxi. Thanks to you, he will get his treatment. May your children live long lives.'

The secretary at the child specialist's clinic took the fee and the doctor proceeded to examine the child.

'But he is dead,' said the doctor on touching the child. Chawali felt as if the ground had shifted beneath her feet. Shakily, she managed to say, 'Doctor what has happened to my child? He just had fever.'

'It seems your child has not died because of a fever but has been poisoned. What did you give him to eat?'

'Nothing doctor, just a little bit of opium to keep him quiet.'

A year later, at the silver jubilee celebrations of the movie, A Mother's Heart, a politician commented, 'I congratulate the producer, director, hero and heroine of this film as their film has managed to capture the beating of an Indian mother's heart.'

The Filmi Triangle

Two days are especially significant in a person's life—the day of his birth and the day of his death. In the short life span of a film, too, there are two crucial days—one is the day of the mahurat, a day when colourful, elaborate cards are distributed, and the other is the day when the film is released, which often also becomes the day of its demise.

The mahurat of Mohan Sailani's film *Jawani Mastaani* was organized in a grand manner. A popular star gave the clap for the film, a prominent distributor pressed the button of the camera and a well-known financier was the chief guest.

There were many stars found twinkling among the guests, with the exception of those who were out shooting in London, Shimla or Kashmir. At the mahurat, innumerable boxes of sweets were consumed by the group of extras and bottles of Campa Cola were gulped down by the assistant cameraman and his friends.

Sailani had thought that the financier would be motivated by the event, so he had invited a big producer, so that the

'Bombay territory' would be allotted to him. But when these distinguished guests found out that the film was launching two new, unknown faces as the hero and heroine, their enthusiasm quickly died out. The hero had made a name for himself in Marathi films, but the heroine was completely new. She was the step-granddaughter of a yesteryear actor and had run away from home. Even though this girl used to address the actor as Nana, her maternal grandfather, everyone knew that she was someone else's child. She was also quite ordinary to look at, so her entry was not going to create any ripples in the film world.

Sailani wiped his brow when the mahurat concluded. His production manager informed him that the event had him cost Rs 2000—Rs 300 had been paid to the studio as rent, Rs 100 was spent on the bottles of Campa Cola, Rs 50 was paid to the fake pandit, who was actually an extra and would often play the role of a pandit in films. There were several photographers present at the event, who kept pressing the flash repeatedly but ended up not taking a single photograph because there were no photogenic faces among the guests. Yet the production manager pocketed Rs 100 on account of their transportation expenses. Out of the 500 rented chairs, most remained empty, but the manager collected Rs 500 on their account as well, even though he had hired them at a cost of Rs 250. The car driver who had accompanied the star who had conducted the ceremony claimed Rs 50 for petrol and a general tip. 'That has to be paid,' the production manager said by way of an explanation.

In order to claim the Rs 2000 from the financier, Sailani had already spent Rs 200, and the production manager rattled off the accounts for the remaining Rs 1800. And now, Sailani had only Rs 50 left in his pocket. Out of this, Rs 25 each was given as taxi fare to the hero and heroine because, at least on this day, they had to be treated respectfully. Finally, only an 8 anna coin was left in his pocket. He tried to pay the bus fare with it, but the driver flatly refused, and so, Sailani had no choice but to walk home.

On reaching home, his wife greeted him angrily, 'I had told you this morning itself that if you did not bring refined oil, no rotis will be made today.' In response, Sailani recounted the expenses incurred during the day, saying, 'Now there is only one 8 anna coin left. You can do what you like with it. Whether you cook rotis or not, I am going to rest for a while.'

With this, Sailani lay down on his bed and started thinking about his film. There was a calendar hanging on the wall that caught his eye, and he gazed at the date: 13 April. It was the most auspicious day of the year, which had prompted him to fix the mahurat of his film on that day. The fake pandit had assured him that the date would maximize his chances of the film completing a silver jubilee.

Heartily cursing the 'fake pandit' in his heart, Sailani fell asleep. He started to dream that the photograph of Lakshmi Paskar, the heroine of his film, had appeared on the front page of *Screen*. Upon seeing the photograph, the financier readily agreed to give him Rs 10 lakh with interest of just Rs 2 lakh. Meanwhile, the broker Chapsi Bhai came to him and said, 'Yaar, I have been searching for you high and low. At least on the day of the mahurat, we should have sat together and had a few cups of coffee. And you chose this day to disappear when the distributors are anxiously looking for you!'

On hearing this, the financier said haughtily, 'I hope the distributors don't give up on you after the long wait. Go quickly and sign the contract with them.' Sailani left with Chapsi Bhai soon after. On the way, Chapsi Bhai said, 'Yaar, please give me a Rs 5 note. My wife had given me Rs 5 which I spent while waiting for you at the coffee house.' Sailani fumbled around in his pockets and among some jingling coins found two Rs 5 notes. He handed one over to Chapsi Bhai. On reaching the distributor, he found that he, too, was intently studying the front page of *Screen*.

'So, Mohan Bhai, where did you find this girl?'

'She is Sohan Babu's maternal granddaughter and acting runs in her veins.'

'Then she must have her grandfather's good luck as well.'

'She is certainly lucky, which is why she has appeared in a Mohan Sailani film. Otherwise, which new girl gets a chance like this? You will also be thrilled when you hear the story. Even the title is fantastic—*Jawani Mastani*. It seems like the title of the film has also been named after this girl. Just take a close look, she is *Jawani Mastani* personified!' said Chapsi Bhai.

'So, we should sign it today,' said the distributor.

'This is precisely why I persuaded Mohan Bhai to leave another distributor's office and come here. He was just about to sign a contract with them when I said, "Mohan Bhai, I have just received a call from your home and your wife has suddenly taken ill." I am sorry to say but sometimes one has to lie in order to do a good deed and that's how I managed to wrest him away from that distributor.'

'How much was he offering?'

'What amount were you going to sign on, Mohan Bhai?'

Mohan thought quickly and replied, 'Rs 11 lakh had been decided for a total of eight prints.'

'Only eight prints! Come on, she's a new girl, and if she's lucky, she will give stiff competition to Shabana Azmi and Smita Patel. We will release at least twelve prints simultaneously. If we can get the requisite cinema halls, we will circulate the film in fifteen places but I cannot offer you more than Rs 11.5 lakh.'

'Done,' Mohan replied quickly.

The distributor said shakily, 'But I said there need to be twelve prints of the film. We cannot do business for less than that.'

'You are also paying me Rs 50,000 more, so this is fine by me.'

'Okay . . . so Arjun,' he called out to his clerk, 'make out a contract in Mohanji's name. The name of the film is *Jawani Mastani*, starring Lakshmi Paskar and Vasant Kumar. Who is the music director?'

'Naushad Ali.'

'Who listens to Naushad Ali these days? He has become old. Take Jeevan Lahiri, he makes such melodious songs.'

'Okay. We will take Jeevan Lahiri.'

'Okay, so then, make the contract and we'll attach a cheque of Rs 50,000 along with it. What is the name of your company?'

'Sailani Pictures.'

'Yes, so the name of Sailani Pictures should be included.'

'The publicity will be for a minimum of Rs 2 lakh. That's fine, isn't it?'

'Yes, everything is fine,' murmured Mohan Sailani weakly and waited patiently for the cheque of Rs 50,000 to arrive.

'Mohanji, will you have something hot or cold to drink? Shall I ask for coffee or juice?'

'Juice is fine. Sweet lime with ice.'

The guard went out of the room, returned with three glasses of juice and handed one to each of the three men.

'I told you to put ice in it,' the distributor growled and sent the glass crashing to the floor.

Just then, Sailani opened his eyes. His wife was in the middle of saying, 'Till when will you keep sleeping? Whatever roti is made without oil, just eat it. Don't you have to go to town today?'

During the good old days, Sailani had got a first-class train pass made; it was still valid for another fifteen days. He walked from Andheri to Grant Road and thought to himself that even though that was all a dream, a good dream was considered a good omen. Somehow or the other, business would work out. 'Let me go and ask the distributor who turned on the camera,' he decided.

Sailani reached his destination and saw that the distributor was reading *Screen*. 'Did you see our heroine's photograph?' he blurted out.

'What rubbish! Your heroine? This is the photograph of Miss Zaira Hashmat. What a girl!'

The second angle

Miss Zaira Hashmat was neither a famous person's daughter nor was Zaira her real name. She was not a Miss either. Rather, she had been married to two men.

She adopted the name Zaira during her days as a model in London. When she came to India and started getting roles in movies, she added 'Hashmat' so that it would appear that she belonged to an affluent Muslim family. The 'Miss' tag is something that every film star wishes to retain, no matter how many legitimate or illegitimate children they might have!

Zaira was the daughter of an Anglo-Indian call girl in London who didn't know who Zaira's father was. As a child, Zaira had seen tough times. Her mother would often be working and wasn't there to feed her, so Zaira often went hungry and craved food. At the age of thirteen, she realized that young girls have something highly coveted which first brings you chocolates and toffees, followed by pounds and dollars, and later, other pleasurable items. And so, she became a nymphomaniac and craved a new partner every day. There were times when even two or three men could not satisfy her, and she became addicted, just like one would to alcohol or cocaine. During this time, something else happened—she started to hate men. For her, a man was a beast, capable of one thing alone.

When she came to Bombay, she attracted a crowd of customers, but she was determined to become a film star and had to curb her desires. She was aware that she could easily ensnare a producer, director or actor in her web. And so, she put up an act of being unattainable. She would have lunches, dinners and attend cocktail parties, all with different men, but when the clock struck 12 p.m., she would feign a headache and dutifully return to her hotel room. Many drunk men tried to enter her room, but each time, she reprimanded them for their behaviour and threw them out. She limited herself to only hugging and kissing. People would say of her, 'What a strange girl. Her disposition is that of a prostitute, but her mannerisms are of a virgin.' Posing as the daughter of a nawab from Hyderabad, who had completed her education in London and Paris, she would become all the more demure in front of people from the film industry. Left to her, she wouldn't allow the hugs and kisses either, but she was well aware that she possessed one treasure alone—that of her body—and if she lost that, no one would even pay a pittance for her. And so, on the pretext of being taught Urdu by a teacher, she would remain shut in her room all day long. She meticulously practised the Hyderabadi style in which begums were known to greet people, and learnt to speak chaste Urdu, albeit in an English rather than a French accent so that it would be evident that she had returned from foreign shores.

One day, she found the one whom she was looking for. Ghanshyam, the son of a very wealthy Sindhi businessman, was new to film production. He spotted Zaira at a party and fell head over heels in love with her. But he had the same experience as several others before him. Zaira drank champagne with him till midnight and even allowed him to kiss her when they were alone in the lift, but that was all. He did not get permission to go beyond that. As soon as it was 12 p.m., she shut herself in her room. Lala Ghanshyam knocked at her door, but to no avail. At one point, the hotel staff had to pacify him and take him downstairs.

One day, Miss Lily, Zaira's hairdresser, said to Ghanshyam, 'Ghan darling, I know that you are in love with Zaira. Why don't you cast her as the heroine in your next film? Then she is sure to become yours.'

Ghanshyam consulted the director of his film, Mehmood Khan, who gave his assessment, 'The girl is definitely photogenic. If she can master the language and shed off her English accent, she can do wonders.'

'Do you have a story?' Ghanshyam asked him.

'I don't have one, but Shafique-Adil have a story that will suit Zaira.'

That same evening, the duo was summoned, and they said, 'We have a subject—*The Girl from Paris*—but it has been promised to Zeenat Aman. But if you still need a story, we'll write another one for the right price.'

'Zeenat Aman is getting us Rs 4 lakh from Sanjay Khan.'

'4 lakh?' Ghanshyam repeated in amazement

'But we are not asking you for 4 lakh. That amount has been promised to us by Sanjay Khan and now we'll have to return the advance taken from him as well. We will take Rs 5 lakh from you.'

'5 lakh!' exclaimed Ghanshyam. 'But will you narrate the story to Zaira?'

'Yes, yes, as soon as we get our advance of Rs 1 lakh. You think about that. We also have to get rid of Zeenat Aman.'

'Give me some idea about the story.'

'The idea is . . . think about an Indian girl who goes to Paris to study and has now returned. She mentions Paris at every opportunity but remains an Indian girl at her very core. She falls in love with a raja who wishes to modernize his *riyasat*. The production value will be sizeable. We will have to shoot at Jal Mahal Hotel in Udaipur. I can only narrate this much for now, but you have to keep this to yourself.'

'Of course. No one but Miss Zaira will hear about this.'

'We have only narrated the story because of you, Mehmood Khan,' said Shafique, and Adil nodded in agreement.

A time was fixed with Zaira. A suite was reserved for the story session at Sea Rock Hotel. Preparations were made for tea, and bottles of champagne were stocked in the cupboard so that if the story was passed, the bottles could be popped.

In the evening, Zaira breezed in wearing a Hyderabadi-style dress—tight pyjamas with a long kurta and a silk dupatta that was five and a half yards long—along with matching jewellery. She certainly looked the part of a royal personage. She walked towards them and greeted Ghanshyam and Mehmood Khan in such an elegant manner that they were both floored. As the aroma of her French perfume enveloped them, it seemed she indeed was the 'Girl from Paris' who had appeared before them.

Mehmood Khan narrated the story with embellishments, mentioning only the girl's role and no other.

After listening to the story, Zaira said, 'It's not bad. Is this by Jean Paul-Sartre?'

Ghanshyam answered, 'It's by someone much better than him. What do you think of Shafique-Adil? Their previous film is currently completing its sixtieth week.'

'But what will my family say?'

'What? Who?' asked Ghanshyam.

'My father is no more but my uncle is extremely strict. It will be very difficult to get his permission. Aside from him, my mother has a very conservative outlook as well. She too might not approve of my working in films.'

'When you tell them the terms, they will certainly give their permission. You see, we are quite generous when it comes to money.'

'We'll offer you Rs 2 lakh.'

'No, no.'

'Okay, Rs 3 lakh, just for you.'

'Okay,' said Zaira half-heartedly. 'But where will I stay?'

'Wherever you wish—in a hotel or at my house. I will get an entire block reserved for you.'

'Oh Allah! What will people say? I will stay at a hotel. I have heard that the Rajput suite at the Taj is good. You can go ahead and make preparations for that.'

'Whatever you wish.'

'And the advance payment?'

'Here it is, Rs 50,000.'

'If you accept it, I shall be much obliged,' said Mehmood Khan with an elaborate gesture.

'Okay, so when will the mahurat of the film be held?'

'Whenever you wish.'

Zaira thought for a while, 'It's my birthday next week.' In reality, she did not even know the actual date when she was born, and so she just picked a random day in the coming week. 'But it's too soon. Wouldn't that create any trouble for you?' she added.

'No, not at all,' said Ghanshyam. 'Mehmood Khan, take out the contract. The auspicious time is here. After that, open the bottle of champagne.'

And so, a grand mahurat was organized where all the well-known celebrities from the film industry were in attendance. It was winter so everyone was in town and not busy with outdoor shoots in Europe or Kashmir. The clap was given by Deep Kumar and Khanpat Rai turned on the camera.

The mahurat was held in Taj Mahal Hotel so that the guests could have their fill of food, whiskey and champagne.

At night, Ghanshyam paid the bill and walked over to the reception.

'Congratulations, Mr Ghanshyam, on the spectacular mahurat. Your heroine is simply one in a million. This message has arrived for you.'

Ghanshyam nervously read the message, 'Come up and see me sometime.'

Ghanshyam could barely contain his excitement and willed the lift to move faster as he hurriedly made his way up to the room. When he reached the suite, he found the door open.

'Welcome home, my darling.'

Thus, Zaira became a star and kept ascending the ladder of success.

The third angle

Everybody was aware that Radhika's mother was a famous star from Andhra Pradesh. But there was some doubt about who her father was. Some said he was a political leader, but a few people thought he was a minister who had also been a film star.

It was said that Radhika came to Bombay at the age of thirteen, though she acted in a film only when she was tall enough to rest her head on a grown man's shoulders. It's hard to imagine that a thirteen-year-old girl could do that. However, there is no doubt that she had the most enchanting eyes. She could captivate anyone with just one look. Like Zaira, Radhika too desired male company, but unlike Zaira, she could be in a relationship with the same man for some months or even years. She had taken on around twelve partners in ten years and preferred big, strong men who were older to her. Only they could physically satisfy her. Thus married producers, directors and senior actors would often become her prey. Sometimes, just as a palate cleanser, she would fall in love with young men. She also enjoyed clandestine relationships with married or engaged men. She was quite brazen about her relationships. Once, she fell in love with a young singer and would dutifully take a tiffin box to the recording studio during the lunch hour and lovingly feed him. Never mind who watched!

Radhika would keep several *mangalsutras* handy in her bag, not knowing when they would be needed. During outdoor shoots, when she would spot a temple, she would catch hold of her current suitor, head to the temple and get married in accordance with the Gandharva marriage tradition. She would dutifully place a mangalsutra around her neck, put a vermillion mark in the parting of her hair and walk away joyously. If anyone asked her if she had got married yet again, she would reply, 'It's nobody's business but mine. I can get married any number of times. After all, even Draupadi had five husbands and Krishna had thousands of *gopis*!'

Miss Lily was the hairdresser of both these women and would inform them about the presence of any young, strapping man on the horizon. One day, she informed Radhika about a strapping, young new actor from Pune who had just started working in Marathi films. At the time, Radhika was involved with a big-time actor, so she quietly made a mental note of this new boy. Coincidentally, Lily had also told Zaira about the same boy. Zaira was involved with a producer-director in those days and the rumour was that she had married him as well.

Then one day, Lily told them both, 'That Marathi boy is working in some Hindi film now. You'll like the title, it's called *Jawani Mastani*.'

'Whose film is it?' asked Radhika.

'Some small-time producer. The film has been put on hold for the past three years because he has run out of money.'

'Tsk, tsk, that's terrible. That wretched producer deserves his fate but it's terrible for the poor actors to have a film stalled for three years! What do you say?'

'What else can you expect? The film is three-fourths ready, and the producer says he can finish everything within Rs 50,000.'

'I don't have Rs 50,000 but ask him if he can work with Rs 25,000,' said Radhika.

Zaira had the same response on hearing this woeful story. But she had one condition. 'First, show me his photograph. If I like the boy, then you can take Rs 25,000 from me.'

The hairdresser brought out his photograph. It was a still from *Jawani Mastani*. The boy was dressed in a red vest and blue jeans. His look, with his tousled hair and muscular arms, was to die for.

'He will do,' Zaira said.

Both Radhika and Zaira took out Rs 25,000 from their stash of black money and handed it to the hairdresser. The hairdresser deducted Rs 5000 as her fee and handed over Rs 20,000 in two instalments to Mohan Sailani, saying, 'Keep this. This money has been given by two film stars who want to help new and upcoming artists and don't want to see their film getting stalled. You finish your work and organize a grand premiere for the film. On that day, I will introduce you to these stars.'

Sailani could not believe that this magnanimous gesture had come from the industry that was widely thought to be inhumane, cold-blooded and stony-hearted. At that moment, he felt that there was no one kinder and more compassionate than film stars. During his dire hour of need, he had been handed over the money without any interest, any receipt or signature. With the money in hand, he quickly organized the shooting as well as the dubbing and recording. Now, he could relax and wait for the premiere.

The three angles

The premiere of *Jawani Mastani* was held in a small theatre but with a lot of pomp and show. Although Sailani had sent out invitations to all the big stars in the industry, he didn't really expect many of them to turn up. But that same hairdresser walked up to him and said, 'Now, at last, let me reveal the names of your benefactors. They are Miss Zaira and Miss Radhika. Both of them are willing to attend the premiere but on the condition that they both should be seated right next to the hero.'

'What is the problem in that?' Mohan said while scribbling the names of Radhika and Zaira on two invitation cards. 'Every person has a seat on either side—one to the left and the other to the right. We'll seat Miss Zaira on the left and Miss Radhika on the right. That should solve the matter.'

The hairdresser collected the invitation cards for Zaira and Radhika, along with her own. She had been assigned a seat in the row right behind the actresses.

When other film stars heard that Zaira and Radhika were both planning to attend the premiere, they started coming in one by one, and soon, the entire hall was packed. There was no place left even in the parking area. All the stars came in their big cars and it became quite difficult to accommodate everyone; the police had to be called to sort it all out. All eyes were fixed on Vasant Kumar, who was looking quite dapper in a suit. If he looked as good on screen, he would create quite a stir. The producer and distributor started discussing his fate in hushed tones.

Zaira walked in first. She located her seat and introduced herself to Vasant, 'You are Vasant, I presume. I am Zaira. You might have seen me on the screen.'

Vasant said excitedly, 'Of course. You were fabulous in *Neeli Deewarein*. There was this scene in which you played a blind girl, and I was just stunned.'

'But Vasant, I am not actually blind,' said Zaira.

'Of course, that is evident,' replied Vasant. 'You have such big eyes that . . .'

'That you are afraid. Is that what you were going to say?'

Written by K.A. Abbas, *Awara* (1951) became an overnight sensation in South Asia, the Soviet Union, East Asia and the Middle East. 'Awara Hoon' rang through Moscow's streets as 'Бродяга я. (*Bradyaga Ya*)'—the song of youth all over the USSR.

Raj Kapoor and Nargis starred in *Anhonee* (1952). K.A. Abbas made this film on Nargis's *farmaiysh*. She played a double role, a first in Indian cinema, in this intense psychological drama.

Rahi (1953), starring Dev Anand and Nalini Jaywant, was based on Mulk Raj Anand's 1937 novel *Two Leaves and a Bud*. It highlighted the repression of the tea garden workers of Assam and their ultimate triumph over their oppressors.

The first songless film of Indian cinema under the Naya Sansar banner, *Munna* (1954), also called *The Lost Child*, was made by Abbas. In this film Master Romi played the 'hero' along with Abbas stalwarts like Jagdeep, Manmohan Krishna, David, P. Jairaj, Tripti Mitra, Sulochana Chatterjee, Madan Puri, Johnny Walker, Achala Sachdev and Rashid Khan.

The first Indo-Soviet production under the Naya Sansar banner and the Soviet state-owned Mosfilm Studio, *Pardesi* (1957), released as *Хождение за три моря* (*Journey beyond Three Seas*) in Russian, was jointly directed by K.A. Abbas and Vasili Pronin. This is an indoor shooting scene in Moscow, with Prithviraj Kapoor seated on the chair and Oleg Strizhenov standing in front of him. On the left, Abbas is sitting on the floor with his assistant director Hamid Sultan standing behind him.

Abbas's best-known political documentary, *Chaar Shehar Ek Kahani* (1968), was given an A certificate by the Central Board of Film Certification because it showed a red-light area and a sex worker. Abbas fought the case up to the Supreme Court and won. This shows him holding up the U certificate which was finally awarded to the film.

Char Dil Char Rahein (1959), Abbas's first multi-starrer made under the Naya Sansar banner, framed the social issues of caste and class through four stories of four individuals which intersect at the crossroads, quite literally. It was a bittersweet experience, with some stars filing cases against him. Abbas vowed never to produce a multi-starrer again.

Abbas attended the second World Youth Congress in 1938 at Vassar College, Poughkeepsie, New York (USA), during his 'Duniya ki Sair' recorded in his travelogue, *Musafir ki Diary*.

At nephew Anwar's *valima* (standing, left to right): Inder Raj Anand, Abdur Rahman (secretary), Prithviraj Kapoor, Ahmad Fatima (Abbas's sister), K.A. Abbas, Krishna Kapoor and Ghanshyam (assistant). Seated (left to right): An unknown child, Shyam Anand (Abbas's rakhi sister), Anwar Abbas, Nadira Abbas, Jafar (crew member) and Anamika Saxena (niece).

Anwar's valima (left to right): Ghanshyam, Anwar Ali (brother of actor Mehmood),
Amitabh Bachchan and an unknown guest.

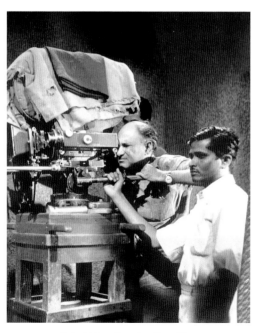

K.A. Abbas shooting for a film.

K.A. Abbas on the location of a film shoot.

K.A. Abbas at home working on a script, Philomena Lodge on Church Road
(now named after him), Juhu (Bombay).

Saat Hindustani (1969) featured the comradeship of seven young people from all over India who came together in a heroic attempt to liberate Goa from the Portuguese colonial rule.

'No, I was going to say that they are bewitching.'

'Thank you.'

'Hello, Vasant,' Radhika's voice came from the right. 'Who is this sitting next to you?'

'Miss Radhika, you don't know her? This is the famous film star, Miss Zaira Hashmat.'

'Hello,' said Radhika icily.

'Hello,' answered Zaira, adopting an even frostier manner. 'How come you are here?'

'Just like you are here.'

'But I didn't know you were allotted this seat.'

'Well, someone or the other has to be seated here. This isn't a box that can be reserved for just the two of you.'

'Hmphh,' grunted Zaira.

'Hmphh,' answered Radhika.

Both of them stood up to show off their sarees and pose a bit so that everyone could spot them easily. Just then, the lights started to grow dim and they both sat down in such a manner that one of their knees was touching Vasant's left knee and the other's his right! He was stuck in the middle, squashed between the two.

'If these seats aren't spacious, should I go and sit somewhere else?' he said and moved as if to get up. Just then, Radhika grabbed his right hand and pulled him down, while Zaira grabbed his left hand and did the same, and the poor chap's hands became captive. The screen lit up and Vasant Kumar's name appeared in the titles. Immediately, the two of them let go of his hands and started clapping. Other audience members followed their lead. When Lakshmi Paskar's name appeared, the two stopped clapping.

'Why do you work with such unknown stars?'

'Because no famous star is willing to even talk to me.'

'But you have never approached me,' said Radhika.

'I had but your bodyguard kicked me out.'

'I shall dismiss him tomorrow itself.'

'I am really sorry . . .'

'But you went to the wrong place, you see. Why didn't you come to Zaira Villa?'

'I went there too but your guard refused to even take my card and give it to you.'

The film started and the audience seemed to enjoy it. The comedy was a bit different, and the hero and heroine were quite lively. There were fewer songs than usual but the ones that were there were appreciated. In fact, the atmosphere was charged with excitement at the presence of so many stars from the industry, and this contributed to the way the film was received.

But three members of the audience didn't really watch the film closely. One was Zaira, who was more interested in staring at Vasant's face despite the pitch darkness of the hall. The other was Radhika, who, instead of watching the screen had turned right and, along with Vasant, was also keeping an eye on Zaira.

The third person was Vasant, who was caught between the devil and the deep blue sea. Zaira's knee was pressing against his from one side and Radhika's from the other. His hands were in the grip of the two women. He tried to wrest his hands out on the pretext of wiping the sweat off his brow but they both held on so tightly that escape was impossible! After a while, he resigned himself to his fate and thought of catching a few winks while sitting there. But that was not to be either. He felt an insect crawling up his right leg and tried to swat it. But it turned out to be Radhika's hand. On his left leg too, he felt the same sensation, and he understood that it was Zaira's hand.

He finally found some respite during the interval. Some
people from his film unit came by and he greeted them
warmly. One distributor congratulated him and said, 'Well
done, Vasant,' upon which his friend commented, 'Well done,
Vasant! You have given a great performance on the screen but
seem to be giving quite another here in the hall too.'

Vasant turned towards the screen and sat down.

'These friends of yours are very ill-mannered. Do they not
have any wives or sisters?'

'That they do but they don't have a girlfriend!'

Sailani walked by clutching a few bottles and said to him,
'So, have you seen how well the editing has highlighted your
performance?'

'Yes, boss,' Vasant replied.

Sailani handed him a cold bottle and said, 'I hope you are
enjoying your seat.'

'It's good but . . .', said Vasant looking around.

The lights started to go dim. They handed the bottles
over to the waiter and the two ladies once again took custody
of his hands. But this time around, at least there were no
creepy-crawlies climbing up his trousers. His friends' remark
at least ensured that. Both women were a bit restrained
because they knew the film would end soon. After that, the
night was theirs alone.

The film got over and people applauded it. Radhika turned
to say something to her hairdresser. Seizing the opportunity,
Zaira congratulated Vasant and extended her hand to shake
his. Without letting go, she hastily led him outside, without
giving him the opportunity to even say goodbye to Radhika.

'Which one of these is your car?'

'Um, I'll take a taxi. I have to go to a friend's place.'

'Even on a day like today? Today is the night to celebrate. Come with me.'

She opened the door of her car and instructed the driver, 'Get us out of this mess and take us to Sea Rock Hotel.'

Vasant reluctantly got in and, as soon as he shut the door, they were off. What was the point in arguing with this young woman, he thought. The film had been appreciated by the audience, and he thought they'd have a celebration at Sea Rock. She would offer him drinks and he'd have a few. What was the harm in that? And after the celebrations, he would go to Lakshmi's house, nearby at Matunga.

The car was speeding along Worli. So far, Zaira had not tried anything sneaky and was sitting in her corner off the car. At the cinema hall, she had only been trying to make Radhika jealous. She extended her hand to Vasant and said, 'Now you have become a star. Just wait till tomorrow and you'll see the reviews praising your performance. Promise me that you will sign your next film with me.'

She said this in a purely platonic manner and shook his hand. Vasant did not respond to her request and kept quiet. He had already promised Lakshmi Paskar that they would work in the next film together, after which they planned to get married. Then Lakshmi would retire from films and take care of the household. Lakshmi had said to him, 'This film has been made with great difficulty. I didn't quite enjoy it. We'll do one more film together and then I will bow out from films and just take care of your home.'

'You didn't answer me,' she admonished him in a friendly tone.

'I don't know what to say. I have already promised to do the next film with someone else.'

'With whom?' asked Zaira enviously, 'With Radhika?'

'No, no. I only met Radhika today along with you, so how could I have promised her?'

'Then with whom?'

'Lakshmi Paskar. You see, we worked together in our first film.'

'Oh, Lakshmi!' She remembered the wheatish-complexioned, ordinary-looking girl, who looked even less remarkable without make-up, and felt relieved that she couldn't hold a candle to her.

She held Vasant's hand and said, 'It is different when it's about Lakshmi. She needs you to star in a film with her, but you can star alongside anybody. Promise me that after completing the film with Lakshmi, you will do the next film with me.'

'But first some producer should decide to cast me, only then can I make these decisions.'

'It is my responsibility to send a producer to you. You only have to say yes,' said Zaira.

'Really?'

At that, Zaira brought her lips close to his ear and gave him a friendly kiss.

They arrived at Sea Rock Hotel. The driver opened the door and, with Vasant's hand in hers, Zaira entered the hotel triumphantly. There were a couple of photographers around who immediately got to work, and their flashbulbs started going off in quick succession. Zaira had called them there but on seeing them, she feigned irritation, saying, 'You people really trouble me but anyway, it's good that you are here. From now on, you'll need to take lots of pictures of Mr Vasant. From today onwards, he too is a star.'

'Good luck, Sir,' said one photographer and dashed out.

They took the lift and reached the suite that was permanently reserved for her. She reached to take out the room keys but found to her astonishment that the door was already open. Radhika's raucous laugh reached her ears, 'Hello, my dear Zaira! You really make your guests wait too long. Come and see who is here with me. Your dear Ghanshyam, along with your secretary. Now, what's your plan? Why don't you make yourself comfortable here while I take Vasant out for a bit.'

Vasant's bewildered eyes moved from one to the other. He could not understand what was going on and what it had to do with him.

'You bitch,' said Zaira through clenched teeth.

'After all, you have shown your true colours, slut.'

'Whom are you calling a slut? Your whole family is filled with sluts.'

With this, they both pounced on each other, and Vasant just about managed to escape with his life. He took the lift, came out, hailed a taxi and asked the driver to start the meter.

'Sir, where do you want to go?'

'Matunga.'

Vasant reached home and found Lakshmi waiting for him. He said, 'Sorry, Lakshmi, it took me a while to get home.'

'What happened?'

'I will tell you later. Suffice to know that I met two witches and have just managed to escape from them.'

'I noticed those two beautiful witches sitting next to you. Thank god that you managed to get away.'

'I have kept the taxi waiting. Come.'

'We'll go but first let's at least have a cup of coffee. Where do you want to go?'

'We'll go to Juhu.'

'It's 2 a.m. We won't be able to sleep till we read what the morning papers have to say about the film, so we might as well stay up.'

Lakshmi finished her coffee and said, 'Let's go.'

There was no light in the staircase as they made their way out of the building. Lakshmi was walking behind Vasant when suddenly her foot slipped and she fell into Vasant's arms.

He bent down and tenderly kissed her and said, 'Congratulations, Lakshmi, our film is a hit.'

Lakshmi replied, 'May this wish come true.'

Parineeta Kumari's Paans

Parineeta Kumari's paans were spoken about in the same manner as people spoke about Cleopatra's nose. Like 'Laazim o Malzoom', as in correlated.

People said, 'Look at that! These whims of film stars. Nothing less than Rs 20 worth of paan in one day! As for taste in food, at least two chickens for two meals.' But those who knew her also knew that she only ate one thing, paan. A spittoon accompanied her everywhere. Its keeper was her friend, hairdresser and confidante Gul Bano. She presented it to Parineeta every few minutes, who bent over and delicately spat in it.

Her husband's name was Nirmal Kumar Sarhadi but he was not from the Sarhad in the North West Frontier Province; he came from a village in District Basti in UP, located next to the Nepal border. That was enough reason for him to attach Sarhadi to his name! When they arrived in Bombay, he was thin as a reed. But when his wife rose to the top and became 'Lakshmi' Devi of pure gold, it all changed in a flash! Doctors, nurses, medicines, hospitals, treatment. A few months of super care changed the man . . . inside out!

People said the two were deeply in love.

Nirmal Kumar Sarhadi, a man of poetic temperament, began with writing lyrics for film songs but soon moved to writing dialogues, and then came the stories. Finally, he started his very first, his very own film venture. The film had Parineeta Kumari in the lead role, and took a long time to complete. At last it was released, and it became a superhit. People said that Nirmal Kumar Sarhadi's total metamorphosis was because of Parineeta Kumari. From being thin, he became fleshy. And Parineeta? At the start, it was she who was fleshy. Then slowly she began losing weight. People remarked, 'She is a saree-wrapped bamboo!' But everyone agreed that she was a stunning beauty. One close-up on screen was enough to send the audience into a trance. And her talent was unparalleled, especially her emotional scenes! Tears flowed down her cheeks without the help of glycerine. She would dissolve in peals of laughter as soon as the shot would be over.

People said Nirmal Kumar Sarhadi was a born artist and poet. A person such as him needed *tanooh*, multiplicities, in life. Perhaps he was becoming tired of Parineeta. His only obsession was to make her work harder and harder so more money could be pulled in from producers. As for Parineeta, she had a shelf which was filled with every award of the film industry. But all she wanted to do was eat paan and write poetry. Her poetic name was 'Raana'. Her poetry was quite mediocre, but each line was filled with pain.

A journalist once asked: 'Why do you compose poetry?'

'For my own satisfaction.'

'Can't you get your satisfaction from Nirmal?'

'Get your answer from him, not from me.'

But the fact was that Nirmal had got a *ghatin*. Parineeta had sent her to him, to wash his clothes. From washing clothes in the bathroom, she had moved to his room to massage his legs and then moved further . . . to his bed.

This relationship was neat and orderly. No scandal, no gossip in the film tabloids.

It was around this time when Parineeta's cough started. Perhaps it was asthma; then her stomach became distended. Someone suggested a paan after meals as a relief. That's where it all began: from one paan to two, until even a dozen were not enough. The intoxication of tobacco-laden paan and the pain of withdrawal—only those who have tasted know!

Every hero who worked with her became infatuated with her, even Ajit Kumar. Ajit Kumar's wife was very beautiful so people thought at least he would not fall for her.

'How shall I thank you?' Ajit asked, taking the packet of paan from her.

'One paan, one kiss. Is that a deal?'

When he bent to kiss her, she turned away and presented her cheek.

'*Janam.*' In private, he always called her 'janam'. 'What does this mean?'

'Whatever you think.'

'You have pyorrhoea? Your mouth smells?

'Whatever you think.'

'Use Forhans toothpaste or suck on Chansitan drops.'

'I have tried them all. The smell persists.'

He kissed her long and hard—and bit her cheek. Looking at the mirror, she said, 'You are very naughty.'

The cough started as soon as he left her make-up room. She asked Gul Bano to bring the spittoon. The bout of coughing was relieved only after she brought out a big red gob.

Now Parineeta became known as a 'harjai', a slut. Any hero who worked with her claimed to be her lover and boasted that he had reached her pinnacle!

The fact was that she allowed kisses only on her cheek, forehead and eyes. Only Nirmal Kumar Sarhadi had enjoyed the pleasure of kissing her lips. This pleasure he had given up many years ago. He was making do with the ghatin.

Anmol Kumar

Sandeep Kumar

Chaman Dehlavi, writer

Bhajan Kumar

Biju Chatterji

The list of her current and ex-lovers was becoming longer.

However, there was one man who had replaced them all. Dr Bhaskar. The doctor had returned with an MD from the US. She had heard about his excellent reputation and also that he was young and good-looking. When her secretary went to fetch him, he refused. 'Film star or whatever she is. If she wants me to treat her, she should come here.' Despite his foreign qualifications, he had decided to work in the municipal hospital. His patients were people from all economic strata; there was no special ward for the wealthy.

When Parineeta, clutching her paan box, climbed the stairs to his clinic, she was out of breath. The place did not even have a lift.

One glance was enough to reveal her condition. She stood before the X-ray machine, her clothes coming off easily. A small skeleton stood before the equipment. Gul Bano had been sent out of the room.

Bhaskar asked, 'You know what your ailment is?'

'Yes.'

'What?'

'One lung is affected by TB.'

'Both lungs. Why have you not taken treatment?'

'I don't want to live.'

'Taking the long road to suicide?'

'Exactly.'

'It's not only TB. Your heart is also affected. One valve has shrunk. Only a quarter of the required blood is being pumped into your body. We may have to operate. You are a big star; will you get admitted in this modest hospital?'

'Only if I can get a private room.'

'No, you can't. You will have to stay in the general ward. You can easily find another physician. He will kill you in luxury. I am ready to kill you for free.' Parineeta burst out laughing.

'You are talking of my death as if you have decided it's a waste of time to save this wretch.'

'Not at all. I am not God but I will try my damnedest to save you.'

'This is an old dialogue from my film *Najma.*'

'It may be that. I saw the film before leaving for the US. What's in your mouth?'

'It's only my spit from the paan.'

'Spit it out.'

'Ask for the spittoon.'

'No, I won't.' He took out a handkerchief from his pocket and spread it out. 'Spit on this.'

She hesitated, then spat.

Half of the red was paan, half was blood.

'How many paans do you chew in a day?'

'Well, about a hundred, maybe more.'

Bhaskar examined the red mess on the handkerchief.

'In your condition, chewing tobacco is poison for you.'

'Exactly. This is why I do it. To stop people from suspecting my disease, I always keep paan in my mouth.'

'You are a strange character.'

Parineeta felt a fondness at the doctor's innocence.

'Yes, that's me. Ask anyone in the film industry.'

'I am only interested in your treatment, that is all.' The doctor firmly put up his medical guard.

'Oh, come on! This is just the beginning of our relationship.'

'So, can you get admitted today?'

'If I said tomorrow, would you mind?'

'The sooner you come the better it will be for you.'

'Then definitely tomorrow. I have to buy enough stock of paan.'

'I will tell them not to allow you a single paan.'

'Whose order is this?'

'Mine, and that's the only order that works here.'

'That even I know, Doctor!'

The next day, Parineeta entered the general ward of the hospital. No film star had ever been admitted to a municipal hospital. Photographers and journalists thronged at the gate. The buzz was that this was democracy at work; Parineeta in a *sarkari* hospital.

There was a veranda in front of the general ward. Dr Bhaskar ordered that blinds be placed there and a curtain installed so that it could become a separate room.

The very first day, the doctor placed an elderly nurse on duty and ordered her to make sure that no one brought paan for the patient. Parineeta tried every trick in her profession to tempt her guardian nurse.

'Get me just one paan, sweetheart, just one, and I will give you this Rs 100 note.' The woman was very tempted but it was time for the doctor's rounds.

When Bhaskar came, he examined the spittoon and sent the red stuff around its edges for a lab test. The test result said 'tuberculosis'.

The brightness on Parineeta's face had been due to the careful application of paint and powder. Now she looked as pale and worn out as other patients in the ward. In two days, even her old producers and directors could not recognize her.

Dr Bhaskar was brutally frank. 'You don't have one, you have three illnesses.'

'What is my first illness?'

'Tuberculosis.'

'Second?'

'Insufficient cardiac function. Your heart is pumping insufficient blood.'

'Third?'

'Chewing tobacco and betel nut has given you cancer of the throat.'

Parineeta burst out laughing and kept laughing until her eyes watered. 'How dramatic! How very dramatic! Cancer and untreatable cancer.'

'But this cancer can be treated. So, we will begin treatment now. And remember, no chillies, no spices.'

From that day, the food hamper from her house was cancelled, and she was offered simple hospital food. Plain dal, plain roti, nothing more.

She refused to eat.

The next day the tray came with the same dal-roti but along with it came Dr Bhaskar.

'Start eating. I want to see you eat.'

With great difficulty, she took one morsel. Then came a glass of milk, which she gulped hungrily.

'That is a good sign. You have taken the first step towards health. Tobacco has killed your appetite.'

At night, Nirmal Kumar arrived at the hospital gate along with press photographers. What a wonderful story! Big star admitted in a general ward! Young and good-looking doctor in attendance! We will make him stand on one side of the bed and Nirmal Kumar on the other, with the general ward in the background. A real scoop. But the photographers and journalists were stopped at the entrance.

'I am her husband,' said Nirmal. 'You cannot stop me.'

'Nobody is stopping you, but this crowd cannot go inside.'

'Who are you?'

'I am Dr Bhaskar and I am in charge here.'

Nirmal Kumar gave up and went inside with the doctor. Bhaskar left him standing near the bed.

'Hello, darling,' he said in a choked voice. 'Where have you come? I will get you admitted in Breach Candy Hospital. The doctor here is a butcher; he treats all patients like dumb animals.'

'I will get treated only from him; actually, today I feel slightly better. They gave me deep rays today. You know, I have cancer of the throat. All this because of my habit of chewing paan. But guess what, I have quit.'

'Who made you quit?'

Before leaving, Nirmal tried to offer Rs 1000 to Dr Bhaskar, who returned it.

'This won't help in the treatment. Take this money back home.'

The next day, the film gossip column headlines screamed: 'Who is the film star languishing in an ordinary municipal hospital, waiting for a certain doctor?'

One week later, the story was repeated in *Film Scandals* magazine, revealing names of the characters, with the headline, 'Sensational romance of a doctor and a married film star'.

When Nirmal was asked about his film star wife, he said it was just a rumour. Dr Bhaskar flatly refused to give an interview.

That night when he came for his last round, he asked Parineeta, 'Do these press people always write scandalous reports?'

'Yes, they do, but this time you also got caught in their snare. So? How do you feel Dr Sahib?'

'I feel as if I've been pushed into a filthy pond. If one more journalist comes here, I will break his jaw, even if I have to stitch it up myself.'

'I am really sorry, Doctor Sahib.'

'Never mind now. You . . . go to sleep.'

He turned off the light. Parineeta waited, thinking now he would take advantage of the darkness. But the doctor had to see another fifteen patients, so she heard his firm footsteps receding down the length of the ward.

If only someone would bring her a paan at this moment, she would work free in his film, Parineeta thought. She then realized she had sold herself to her husband's company and thereby lost the power to sign her own contracts. In this train of thought she fixed the price of Rs 1 lakh for one paan! But where would she find black money in the hospital? In the jumble of these thoughts she fell asleep . . . thanks to the sleeping pill. When she woke up, the nurse was taking her temperature.

That evening when Nirmal came to see her, Parineeta whispered, 'My love, get me one tobacco paan, very quietly.'

'It's very difficult today, but tomorrow . . . I promise.' The next day, Nirmal managed to smuggle one paan. That night she had a coughing fit and spat out a lot of blood mixed with the residue of the paan.

Bhaskar got the spittoon examined in his office. Then he stormed into her enclosure.

'Hello Dr Bhaskar,' she smiled. Her face was very pale, almost yellow.

'Who gave you this poison?'

'What poison, Doctor?'

'This tobacco paan.'

'Now, now, Doctor, you are getting paranoid. I have not had paan for days.'

'Then what is this?' he said, showing her the red marks on the rim of the spittoon.

'This is blood. Don't you recognize it, Doctor?' Parineeta smiled.

'So . . . you won't tell me. Now I have to tighten the guard around your bed,' he said as he left her side. Parineeta sighed and closed her eyes in exhaustion. The nurse found her drenched in a cold sweat. That night when Nirmal came to see his wife, he was searched, but he had hidden the paan in the folds of his dhoti. Standing beside her, he slipped the paan under her pillow. 'Take this. I had to play with my life to get it. That wretched doctor has placed a guard everywhere. But I can outwit even him!'

In this manner, every day the paans kept arriving. Finally, Dr Bhaskar admitted his defeat and removed the guard.

That night the doctor came to see her.

'Parineeta.'

'Yes, Doctor?'

'Tomorrow you have to be operated. It's a very critical operation. Are you ready? And yes, please don't eat a single paan tonight.'

'All right, Doctor.'

'Good night.'

'Good night.'

As soon as he left, Parineeta reached underneath her pillow. Slowly she placed the tobacco-filled paan in her mouth. She really wanted to enjoy it tonight.

The next morning, when the nurse came to prepare her for the operation, she screamed.

Parineeta was dead.

The doctor came running.

'Parineeta . . . at last you killed yourself . . . you did not give us a chance to save you.'

Then the doctor did something which was very unprofessional. He bent down and kissed her dead lips. That was the time he found out the taste and the fragrance of a paan laced with tobacco. From that day, Dr Bhaskar started chewing tobacco paan every day. This was the only way he had to keep her memory alive in his heart.

Kayakalp: The Rejuvenation

Films have a world of their own, a language of their own; the characters are different from people in our lives.

There is the hero. He may be tall or short, either clean-shaven or with a moustache. It may be long and thin like wings of an airplane. The hero never has a beard. Although to trick the heroine or even the villain, he may wear a false one. For the same reason he 'becomes' a doctor, a barrister or a taxi driver. But he does all this for his love. He is a doctor so that he can treat her or her husband (his rival). He is a barrister so that he can save the heroine from a false charge of murder. He is a taxi driver because the love of his life sits in his car. While he forgets to turn on the meter, she leaves her purse and her heart in the taxi.

Then there is the heroine. She may be slim, she may be plump but hardly ever poor! This is for a reason: she must change her dress for every scene.

Scene number 1: Salwar kameez

Scene number 2: Bharatanatyam costume with a nine-inch 'above navel' choli

Scene number 7: Mini skirt, tight top

If perchance she is a poor man's daughter, she wears a silky ghaghra, tight shirt and nylon dupatta with some white patches. Reason? Her father is under the villain's debt, and she is ready to offer the ultimate sacrifice!

Then there is the villain, in a checked shirt, breeches, riding boots, whip in his hand. Or black sherwani with churidar, rakish cap; on his lips dangles a cigarette in a pure gold holder. Even in the heat of summer the man wears white gloves, black overcoat with upturned collar and a black felt hat pulled over his eyes. Two reasons? Police evasion, they cannot identify him, and his clothes don't hurt any religious sentiment!

Next is the vamp who is also called a 'lady villain'. We hear that, in the early days, heroines wore simple clothes. In contrast, the vamp wore flashy, 'indecent' dresses. Today, when the heroines are dressing in the same 'vampish' style, it is difficult to say who is who! Earlier the vamp used to be a dancer; today heroines are also dancing, at least at their own birthday parties. Under these conditions, the vamp has become inconsequential. Regardless, it is the vamp who entices the hero with song- and-dance numbers such as 'Aa ja' 'Aa gale lag ja'. She dances in the villain's nightclub, is his hired moll, but her heart beats only for the hero. In the last scene when the villain whips out his pistol and shoots the hero, it is the vamp who takes the bullet on her chest. As she falls into the hero's arms, there is a smile on her face, 'At last I have got you.' And then her eyes close forever.

There are other characters too. The side-hero is the hero's friend and side-heroine the heroine's; they are in love with each other. There is the assistant villain, the sidekick of the boss. And you can't forget the comedian and his comic beloved.

But my story is not about them. It is about a 'vamp'.

Her name was Rani Bala. She started with playing the heroine but, for the last eight or ten years, she has been playing the vamp. Her career as a heroine was quite unremarkable but she was a hit as a vamp. For one, she was beautiful and her body was perfect, as if it were poured into her garments. Her eyes were large and expressive, her hair thick and wavy and her breasts were sculpted like the Ellora and Ajanta sculptures.

Rani Bala was so pretty that heroines did not like to work with her. Directors and producers cast her in their films because she guaranteed success. If they cast Rani Bala even with a B-class heroine, the film sold at A-class rates. Heroes loved to work with her because with her on the set, nobody bothered to look at the heroine. Besides, she was good-natured, good company, and she had thousands of anecdotes to tell about the film world. There was, however, one rule. She never talked about her private life, and if a director or producer became insistent and amorous, she cut him off with, 'You have never seen my husband, have you? Boxing champion, wrestler and a 70-inch chest!' After this, no one dared to get close. 'Make me do anything before the camera: strip me, kiss me, I am yours to command. But once off the camera, the one who owns my body is only my husband.'

Whether he was a boxing champion or a wrestler, the fact was that nobody had ever seen him! Rani Bala had never given anyone the chance. 'I don't take the studio home nor do I get my home to the studio.' She was the only one who brought no chaperone, no grandmother, mother, uncle, brother or sister. She never invited colleagues home. Even the studio car driver who came to fetch and drop her could not enter. The minute she heard the horn, she came out holding her make-up box and tiffin, and got into the car. Who was inside, how many people . . . nobody knew. People said maybe there was a child because a studio driver had once heard a child say, 'Bye bye, Mummy.'

During her film mahurat, neither her husband nor her child ever accompanied her. Rani Bala's domestic life forever remained a secret. Also, people could never guess her age. She had been in the industry for fifteen years, so could she be thirty? Thirty-two? In her viewer's eyes, she always looked young. A journalist once asked her, 'Ms Rani Bala, what is your age?'

'How old do I look to you?'

'To me? No more than nineteen or twenty.'

'So I am! Nineteen or twenty! A star is as old or young as she looks to her viewers!'

When she came to the studio, Rani Bala was always elaborately made up. No one had ever seen her without make-up. She had her reasons. 'How a woman appears in her home is her private affair. But when she comes to the studio, she is only an actress; an actress has to be very particular about her face and form. I don't like . . . in fact, I hate actresses who go from party to party all night and in the morning appear in the studio with wild hair, dried lips and dirty eyes. Then the make-up man takes two to three hours, and only then are they able to stand before the camera.'

One day, there was a scene in which the hero and heroine were romancing by the side of a lake. Suddenly the vamp appeared, hid behind a tree and watched the lovers. In a rage, she stepped back and fell in the lake. 'Rani, do you know how to swim? The water is over five feet deep.' The director was pointing towards the lake. 'If I drown, I will take you along with me!' The crew burst into laughter. Rani was proud that she had never said 'no' to enacting any scene. No matter how difficult, she never asked for a double to stand for her. Whether it was a fire, a jump off a wall or riding a wild horse, she did all the scenes itself. At that time, heroes and heroines were required to swim, drive, box, fence, everything. So, she immediately got ready to jump into the water. Before the scene began the director asked the wardrobe man to keep three to four identical dresses ready in case there were retakes.

With the requisite anger, envy and precision, she stepped back and fell into the water. She let out a mandatory scream, showed a clenched fist. The director said 'cut'. She was taken out of the lake; everyone was singing her praises. But the cameraman said, 'Sorry, once more . . . technical flaw.' So she was dried and changed. Once again she fell into the water but once again, there was a 'technical flaw'. Then again and again. Finally, it was an 'okay'. From the lake she walked straight to the make-up room. One assistant director whispered, 'Did you see how her youth was washed off? Momentarily, I could see the wrinkles on her face.'

Rani Bala hurried to her cabin. She looked at the mirror. There it was; she saw what others had seen. Throwing out the hairdresser and make-up man, she banged the door shut. After ninety minutes, when she came out, she looked young like always, although a little flustered. Going straight to the car, she said to the driver, 'Home. I am not feeling well.'

The next day, Rani did not return to the studio. Due to the repeated 'drowning', she had developed a whooping cough. The next day, pneumonia was reported; the doctor suggested going to a health resort. Then came the news that her condition had worsened and she had to be flown to Europe for treatment.

With the shooting postponed, there were conjectures. 'Illness was just an excuse. She is trying to regain her lost youth.

She has a yogi in Benaras who is going to perform *kayakalp*.'
There was another version: 'No. There is a doctor in London,
plastic surgeon, who can make middle-aged women young.
That is where the operation will be done.'

Three months later, when Rani Bala returned to the studio,
she was more beautiful than ever. Whatever it was—plastic
surgery, *kayakalp* or magic—it was a great success. She now
looked no older than eighteen or twenty. One hero, a known
flirt, said, 'Rani, I really want to fall in love again! Now please
don't call me Bhai Sahib.'

'No! I will now call you Uncle,' came the reply. The whole
studio screamed with laughter. The actor was left red-faced.

Rani Bala never used to give such sharp replies. People
noticed the difference. She used to be so cheerful and fun-
loving. But now she had become different—very serious, almost
sombre; if anyone made a trite or light-hearted comment, she
gave a sad smile. Someone said, 'Rani, you have really changed:
so serious and so beautiful? Did you get operated for both?' She
only said, 'This operation not only alters the face, it also alters
the temperament.'

People in the studio wondered why had she become so
serious. 'Look at her face, she doesn't look any more than
eighteen. But she is not a day less than forty. When I was in
school, I used to watch her films. She must be thinking, "I
look young, but everyone knows my age." The very thought
is depressing.'

Even now, Rani Bala came from home with full make-up.
There were more conjectures: 'Her make-up has become very
dark. I think it was neither an operation nor kayakalp. It's the
magic of make-up which makes her young. It's paint-powder;
take away these layers and what's underneath?' the assistant

director said this to the director, who just laughed. 'This time when Rani is thrown into a lake or a swimming pool, let's see if the make-up washes off!'

So, an outdoor shooting was arranged. Rani was happy. 'Thank god, at last we can get out of the studio, and I can breathe some fresh air.' The director said, 'As if this is the first time you have done outdoor shooting! Every year you are out on location for two to three months!' She said quietly, 'But after this operation, this is the first time!'

The water was beautiful and quite deep. Everyone knew that Rani was a swimmer; once she had even saved the hero from drowning. The director explained the scene. 'Rani, the villain is running after you. To save your *izzat*, you jump into the lake. You scream and scream. The hero comes running and jumps after you, but it is too late. He brings your dead body out of the water.'

'Is the water deep?'

'Not very,' the director laughed. 'But you know how to swim, don't you?'

'I know . . . but it's been a long time! You will be there, won't you? In case I need . . . '

'Yes, we will be right here. If you are in the slightest danger, just shout.'

So, the camera was positioned. An assistant cameraman said, 'Today, the secret of Rani's youth will be finally revealed when the water of this lake washes off layers of make-up.' Rani and the villain appeared at the brink of the lake. The director said, 'Okay.' Two cameras were set up—one for the long shot, one for the close shot. 'So that we don't have to retake,' the director explained. The cameras were ready and the director shouted 'roll'. The assistant said, 'Bhola Shankar, scene 13, shot 78.' The clipper boy then moved out of the way and the director said 'action'.

Rani came running for her izzat and life from behind the trees. She went straight to the lake, bent over it and looked back. The villain had come very close, so she threw herself into the lake. The crew stood at the brink, the director said 'Okay'. Suddenly, she came up, threw up her hands and shouted, 'Bachao, bachao, bachao.'

'I am coming,' the hero shouted and jumped into the lake, but before he could reach her, she disappeared. In a few moments, he was bringing her out. It was a very dramatic moment. It appeared she was holding her breath, one of her hands hanging limply at her side. 'Look . . . look,' one assistant said to the others. 'Her make-up had been washed away and behind the layers a more beautiful and young face has appeared. Wonderful, Rani, you have done wonders.'

There was a sudden shout from the hero, 'Oh no! Please . . . please . . . she has fainted.'

The car was driven at a breakneck speed. The door of her house opened. A woman's voice was heard, 'Baby, are you here?' One of the studio hands carried the girl in his arms. Then they saw. An old, paralysed man was lying on the bed and next to him sat an elegant elderly woman who bore a striking resemblance to the girl he was carrying. 'What happened to you, my child?' the woman ran to the sofa where she had been placed. A doctor was summoned. He felt her pulse. 'She is not sleeping . . . she is dead.' The man lying on the bed could neither speak nor move. People noticed tears flowing from his eyes.

'How did this happen?' the woman asked. 'It was a drowning scene,' the director said.

'But she knew how to swim!'

Suddenly the woman went mad. She looked at her own hands and screamed. 'I have killed my child with these . . . my own hands.' She turned to the director. 'This news . . . this news should be killed right here.'

'That is impossible. When the shooting is cancelled, it will become big news.'

'No, the shooting will not be cancelled.'

'But who will who replace her?' Everyone in the room was stunned.

Slowly, precisely, the words were spoken. 'I will take her place. Because . . . I am . . . I am not just . . . her mother. I am Rani Bala.'

Achchan's Lover

I live in a shack near Juhu beach with my fight master and four extras. Every morning before sunrise, I go for a walk on Juhu Chowpatty for my workout. In the beginning I was the only one; slowly a few others started coming. When Juhu's population began increasing, hundreds of women, children and men began visiting the beach—some for yoga, some to worship the sun or any other god, some to drink coconut water. We stunt men used the beach to practise our stunts: sword play, horse riding, *utha patakh*.

Horse riding brings film stars here as well; they take advantage of the predawn hours. It was here I saw Achchan for the first time. He had come with his girlfriend Sulekha for horse riding. Achchan and Sulekha were working in a film called *Raj Kumar aur Raj Kumari*. They made a beautiful pair: Achchan, a six feet tall, well-built youth, and Sulekha a tiny China doll.

Achchan's name was Ashok Kumar, but on account of the hero Ashok Kumar, he had changed his name. At home he was called Ashok, not Achchan. His mother was a Bengali from whom he had inherited his beautiful eyes. His father was a Punjabi army officer from whom he had inherited his features and athletic body. In six to seven years, he had travelled a long distance from the Film Institute in Pune to the heights of stardom. Beginning with a paltry Rs 5000 for his first film, he leapt to Rs 25,000 for his second. After the film's success, he climbed fast. Rs 2 lakh, 3, 4, 5, 6, 7, 8, 9, 10 there was no end—above him was only God and, of course, Amitabh. People said, one day, he would become as big as Amitabh Bachchan. In any case, after Bachchan, there was no one else but Achchan. He was slightly shorter than Bachchan, but even better looking, tall, with broad shoulders. In his grip was Ali Baba's lamp. But even Ali Baba's genie could not match the genie he had captured. After all, Ali Baba had only one Marjeena who was crazy about him. Achchan had thousands of Marjeenas all over the country, eyeing him, ready to devour him in one gulp. He had no cure for his love-sick fans!

In the stunt school, I had just graduated from 'extra' to 'duplicate'. My body was like Achchan's, so along with Dilip Kumar, Shashi Kapoor and Sunil Dutt, I was fit to play Achchan's duplicate as well. There was one problem: Achchan hated using a duplicate. It was only rarely, when a personal shooting was just not possible, that he told the director, 'For this scene, use a duplicate.'

One day, I was practising with our stunt master and fellow stuntmen on the beach behind Hotel Sun n Sands. All of a sudden, Achchan and Sulekha passed by on their horses. Achchan was on a white horse and Sulekha was riding a black one. They were looking fabulous in trousers and sweaters on that winter morning. When the sound of the horses faded, I heard a voice: 'Oh my!'

It was a girl's voice. But there was no girl around. I turned around and saw that it was the smallest member of our team, Inder.

'Hey, Inder . . . you sound just like a girl.'

Just then a hard slap made me stagger and almost fall.

'What's your take on this slap?'

This Inder was a rag! One day, he was seen by our master as the *jamhoora* of an acrobat who was demonstrating yoga asanas. 'See the skills of an acrobat.' He placed two bricks, one on top of the other. He took a third and showed its solid state to all the bystanders. Then he struck it with his palm and broke it in two. The slap which landed on my cheek reminded me of the brick.

That day it was Masterji's birthday, perhaps his fortieth or fiftieth considering he had played Master Vithal's duplicate. Then he played the duplicate of the Billimoria brothers and later of Raj Kapoor and Dilip Kumar. So that day we boys decided to treat ourselves to bhel puri at Juhu beach. There, on the beach, was the acrobat with his waifs. Seeing the little yoga experts, Masterji asked the smallest one, 'Wah, wah! Jhamooray, will you come along with us?'

'Where?' Inder asked.

'The silver screen, where you can go as far as you desire.'

Inder was looking at Achchan's magnificent poster under which was written, 'India's beloved Achchan in his new film *Kismet ka Khel.*'

Without taking his eyes off the poster, he asked, 'As far as Achchan?'

Masterji (no one knew what his real name was. We called him 'master'. On the set he was called Fight Master) replied slowly: 'Yes, son . . . if your kismet clicks . . . I will get you there.'

'Let us shake hands, palms up!' He held out his delicate hand towards Masterji's calloused palm. Masterji never shook hands with us; he feared our hands would be crushed by his thick paw. But today was his birthday. Everyone was in high spirits! He held out his hand to Inder with an indulgent smile. But Inder's grip was so tough that for a long time after we saw Masterji stroking his hand. From that day onwards, none of us dared to shake his hand, nor did we try to trifle or jest with him.

Masterji brought Inder home, and we made place for him in the shack. After that, our entire life changed. Inder did everything—washing and ironing our clothes, cleaning, sweeping, everything that girls normally do. One day Feroz Punjabi, our muscle man, stroked his leg. The blow from Inder was lethal. Never again, he vowed.

Inder was new to stunt fighting. We all tried to give him a crash course in stunt *baazi*. He learnt quickly and was able to wrestle. He could lift each one of us. He knew karate already. What he did not know was pretend fights. This we taught him, also scissors, sword, trip. He was a fast learner . . . eager to get to the top.

There was one problem; no hero was his height and weight. He was ideal for a heroine's duplicate.

That day when he saw Achchan and Sulekha on horseback, he asked, 'Masterji, could I become Miss Sulekha's duplicate?'

'Why not? If there is a need for a duplicate in *Raj Kumar aur Raj Kumari*, I will ask the director.'

'Someday there may be a quarrel between Raj Kumar and Raj Kumari. Then Achchan will be there, but not Sulekha. Then they will need me . . . since Sulekha won't be there!'

Then he clamped up—as if he had spoken too much. I said, 'You seem more interested in working with Achchan than becoming Sulekha's duplicate. That is it, isn't it?'

'Big stars work with big stars,' he said with pride. Somehow, I felt he was more Achchan's rival than Achchan's admirer!

A week later Masterji gave Inder some good news. The next day he would have to act with Achchan as Sulekha's duplicate. For that one shot with Achchan, he would be paid Rs 100.

'Mubarakbaad, Inder, your dream has come true. Give us a treat, man.'

'For getting Rs 100 or for working with Achchan?'

'Both,' we all said.

That night Inder did not sleep a wink. Masterji gave him a sleeping pill to calm him down. The thrill of working with Achchan kept him on edge all night.

The next morning, he was up before any one of us. After a bath, he pulled on his newly washed jeans, wore a silk shirt and wrapped a silk scarf around his neck.

'Man, you will have to take all this off, strip,' someone from our group remarked. When Inder threatened him with a karate chop, he quickly added, 'No need to fly off! I was just saying that you will have to wear Sulekha's ghaghra-choli . . .and stuff the choli cups with cotton.'

'Let us see what happens,' Inder said as he was leaving. 'I will let you go for today . . .today is, after all, a celebration.'

The scene was to be shot in a Juhu building: the heroine—meaning Sulekha, meaning Inder—was being held captive in a balcony which was on fire. Achchan had to swing on a rope to reach her balcony, grab her, and swing back to his own balcony.

Inder was explained the scene. He was given Sulekha's clothes to wear.

Achchan used to perform all his own stunts. He had rehearsed the scene twice on his own. He had swung from one balcony to the other. Thousands of his fans had collected down below, school and college boys and girls, building residents, tourists, passers-by. Today, instead of monkey tricks, they had come to watch Indian film star tricks. Here the famous star (who took a fee of Rs 10 lakh per film) would swing like a monkey from one balcony to the other. From there he would grab his mate (Sulekha aka Inder) and swing back to his balcony. Danger, huge danger. For the fire, a fake balcony was fixed on top of the six-storey building. Going up the lift with Masterji, Inder said, 'Sir, how shall I thank you? You have enabled me to climb so high.'

Masterji patted his back, 'Don't worry, son, God willing all will be well. You just stick to Achchan. The rest I have explained. Achchan will take good care.'

'Don't worry, Sir. I will stick so fast to him . . . he'll never forget.' Masterji left him on the rooftop and returned to the ground floor.

When Inder appeared on the balcony of the sixth floor in costume, people were amazed. Inder looked like a carbon copy of Sulekha, hardly a duplicate. In fact, he was 'sone pe suhaga'. The choli was stuffed with cotton. In the lehnga and choli, he looked every bit a rajkumari. From up there he saluted us, his friends, and waved a 'V' sign.

'At last he has got his heartfelt wish,' I said to the others.

Achchan was gazing at Sulekha (sorry, her duplicate). The real Sulekha was herself on the ground, six storeys below, standing on top of her car, watching the shoot.

The camera was fixed on a crane in a long shot position. The director blew his whistle and his voice echoed on the amplifier, 'Fire.' Fake flames surrounded Inder.

The director's voice boomed, 'Camera.' The cameraman shouted, 'Camera rolling.' The director then shouted 'Achchan' and waved his arms in the air.

Sulekha's recorded voice was heard, 'O please . . .save me . . . save me.'

It was the voice of Sulekha, but the lips of the duplicate moved. Rajkumari, Sulekha's character, was caught in the flames.

'I am coming, Rajkumari.' This was Achchan's voice.

A woman's voice said, 'Come, my love, I have been waiting for a long time.'

The director was furious. 'Who asked this rag to speak? I will take him on later.'

'Here I come.' Achchan swung on the rope. In a moment, he swooped down to the other balcony where Rajkumari, aka Sulekha, aka Inder, was waiting. Beautiful eyes . . . he had seen them somewhere. A photograph? So many girls had sent their photographs. But this one was . . .

He felt a heart pounding under the choli which was pressed against his chest. But this was not cotton; a women's breast.

Inder read the question in Achchan's eyes and spoke. 'I am, after all, your lover, yaar. I had your name tattooed on my breast. Don't believe me . . . see it!'

O god! The shock! It was a girl who was clinging to him. Achchan's hands went limp, the grip slackened. He wanted to say, 'What stunt is this?' But the words were stuck in his throat. The next moment, the girl had left the circle of his arms and was plummeting to the ground.

But Inder felt he was flying . . . very high. Masterji had fulfilled his promise.

'Such accidents happen,' the producer expressed sympathy.

'What a life . . . these stunt actors,' a bystander said.

All of us stunt fighters took our friend's dead body to the hospital for a post-mortem and then for the cremation. After the post-mortem, the doctor asked, 'What was the name?'

'Inder,' Masterji said.

'Inder or Indira. The tattoo on her breast was Indira-Achchan.'

'Breast? It was cotton, Dr Sahib, cotton stuffed in the choli, not breast,' Masterji replied.

The doctor looked at Masterji kindly. His eyes seemed to say, 'Can't a doctor make out the difference between cotton and breasts?'

Actress

When I announced my film *Jago Hua Savera*, lots of people in the filmi *duniya* began to talk about it. People said, 'Khwaja Sahib has announced his last film.' They seemed to imply, 'Let us see if he can complete this one!'

Then the conversation turned to casting. I had chosen the male cast, but the female cast was yet to be selected. Some people thought I would cast Smita Patil while others surmised that I would cast my old friend and neighbour Kaifi Azmi's daughter Shabana. One magazine wrote that I might cast the beautiful Tamil heroine Sundri Devi. I was quite shocked at this suggestion. Shabana and Smita were possibilities, but I could never think of casting a person like Sundri Devi! I had never met her, but I had seen her photographs. She was very beautiful, no doubt. But she was called 'Tamil sex bomb', and that was reason enough I could never think of casting her in my film! In one article, I wrote that even if Sundri agreed to work for free, I would not cast her. I wanted a 'real' woman, not a sex-packed '*kathputli*'.

One day, my doorbell rang and, as usual, without taking my eyes off the newspaper I was reading, I said, 'Come in.' The door opened and a girl entered. I looked and looked hard. I had never seen such a dark complexion before. 'Please sit down,' I said in a mild manner. 'What do you want?'

'I am an actress and I want to work in your new film.' I don't know why but I felt that she chewed every syllable of the word actress.

'Have you ever worked in a film before?'

'No. But I know you like new stars. Did Amitabh Bachchan act in any film before *Saat Hindustani*?'

'He did not. But are you comparing yourself with Amitabh?'

'Why not, what's the harm? Is it only my complexion, Abbas Sahib? But in your film you need a dark-skinned girl, don't you?'

'How do you know?'

'I have read the novel *Jago Hua Savera*. There is only one girl and her name is "Kaali".'

'So, you read Hindi novels? Where are you from?'

'I am from central India, Nagpur.'

'Your name?'

'Are you interested in my work or in my name?'

'I am interested in your work, but I need to know your name.'

'Why?'

'So I can call out to you.'

'When?'

'During the shooting.'

'Then call me "Kaali".'

'Then from today your name will be "Kaali Mata".'

'Do I look like a mata to you?' she snapped.

'Oh no, I was just joking.'

'Then Kaali is enough.'

Somehow, this dark girl was a perfect fit for the role. With her black skin, she was very good-looking. She had large eyes, an aquiline nose and a beautiful body. Her speech was perfect. I thought to myself, I always cast a new artist without a test, so why not her? But before saying a single word about casting, I had to clarify something important.

'If I sign you today, the fee will be very modest. Do you know that?'

'Yes, I know.'

'In *The Naxalites* we could not give any more than Rs 5000 to the artists. Even Smita Patil and Mithun Chakraborty got Rs 5000. We gave the same to everyone in the cast and crew because we believe in equal distribution.'

'Yes, I know, you can give me no more than Rs 5000. And if there is a loss, then give me even less.'

'Are you serious? You are signing the contract without reading it?' I asked her.

'I don't need to read it, but I want to do the role of "Kaali" in your film.'

Kaali's role was the longest and the most difficult in the film. Kaali was a young tribal girl in a big city. She collected residual coal dropped by engines from railway tracks. This was the only work she knew, work which had darkened her face and hands. That's why everyone called her 'Kaali'. In this 'business', she was caught twice by the railway police and sent to jail. She lost her 'job'. Not just that, she was beaten and raped. But she always gave the same statement: 'Sir, I am not guilty. I am innocent. It was not I who was disgraced. The men who raped me butchered their own respect. That is because they violated an innocent woman.'

It so happened that a police constable fell in love with her. She loved him too but refused to hide anything from him. 'What is there to hide when I am with you? I have been caught five times and every time I have been raped. But no matter how my body has been used, my heart is pure. I am innocent. Do you love me?'

The police constable gave a stock answer. 'Yes. No fault of yours.' But in his heart he wondered, 'Is this really true? Is she really as innocent as she claims? She is *kaali* all over; is she kaali at heart too? Is her character spotless? She has been used so often by men, what if she has become habituated to it?'

He asked a friend for advice. The friend advised him to stay away from Kaali: 'The girl is "spoiled", her character is "soiled".'

The constable, whose name was Bhaskar, was torn apart. What should he do? Or what should he not do? This question has evaded the best philosophers of all times. And who was he? Only a nineteen- or twenty-year-old matriculate police constable. How could he grapple with this huge life-and-death question? He stopped meeting Kaali.

Kaali kept walking on her own railway tracks, kept working on her railway tracks.

One day Bhaskar was placed on railway protection duty. That night, he caught Kaali stealing coal.

'What the hell are you doing?'

'Stealing coal,' Kalia said brazenly.

'Do you know this is a crime?'

'I know.'

'So you know you are committing a crime.'

'I know, and I also know that it is difficult to sleep hungry and suicide is not only a crime, it is also a sin. If I don't get food, I will die and so will my old father.'

'Why don't you look for some other work?'

'What work shall I take up? Shall I smuggle Seth Bevdamal's wine bottles from here to there? Or shall I wrap inflated rubber around my stomach and in the guise of a pregnant woman transport liquor from one *bhatti* (brewery) to another? Should I display my youth in a shop window so that buyers can be lured to come, as suggested by many touts? Should I tell you more or is this list enough?'

'Stop, it is enough . . . I have not seen anything . . . get lost . . . go home and do your work.'

It occurred to Kaali that this was the first time in her life that she had seen a beautiful and noble person like Bhaskar.

She asked, 'Are you sure?' Bhaskar smiled and looked at her.

'Why are you laughing?' Kaali asked.

'I was laughing at your nonsense talk. Are you mad?'

'Yes, I am mad, that is precisely why I am standing here talking to a havildar. If this is not madness, then what else is this?'

'You run from here, otherwise I will place the manacle on your wrist.'

'Why don't you do that, Sahib? I will happily wear it if you place it there.' Bhaskar took out the manacle. She extended her hand. He placed the manacle around her hand, rotated the key and then pulled it out. The other manacle was already around his own wrist.

'So, now we are married. When will you go around the holy fire with me?'

'Come you, *saali*, Kaali.'

'Where?'

'Wherever I take you.'

'Thana is not in this direction.'

'I know that. I am not taking you to the thana. I am taking you to my house. This will be your life imprisonment. Tomorrow I will resign from my job because I have married a thief.'

'Really? Say that again.'

'Sure, I'm not afraid of saying I have married a thief.'

A loud whistle blew from the train as if the engine was pleased at what was happening on its tracks.

'Marriage does not happen with a thief. It happens with a woman.'

'So, I married a woman, and this marriage is not with a policeman, it is with a man.' 'Who is the man?' Kaali asked.

'That I will tell you after the *pheras* are over.'

At that moment, the darkness of the night disappeared. A pink streak appeared in the sky as if the night had gifted Kaali a dupatta just as it was receding.

Kali and Bhaskar were walking between the rail tracks bound to each other, manacle to manacle, but this was the manacle of love and a metaphor of the days to come.

This was the last scene of the film.

When this last scene was being shot, Bhaskar, the hero, looked at her wrist. Where the manacle had been placed, there was a white streak. He whispered in Kaali's ear, 'The cat is out of the box.'

'Oh, keep quiet.' Kaali whispered. 'Let the last shot be over.'

'Okay, let it be over.' They spoke in conspiratorial tones.

When the scene was shown on the screen, the entire hall rose up in standing ovation. For the first time, the film was being shown in a projection hall. All the artists, the technicians, the press and friends were packed all the way from the screen to the door. When this huge crowd moved outside, I breathed a sigh of relief. My hard work had paid off. The entire audience was praising Kaali. But she was hiding somewhere in the darkness.

'Kaali, come here,' I said.

In response, a bouquet of roses was placed in my hand. Then I felt a young woman's body brush against my own. And the next moment, Kaali placed her lips on my cheek. Just as well that this happened in the dark. Hence, except for a few, no one saw it. When I returned home, I saw my face in the mirror. There was the mark of lips on my cheek. But instead of red lipstick, it was a black mark. On the table next to the bouquet of flowers was a card on which were written the following words:

'Namaste, Abbas Sahib.

In future don't reject a star only for the crime of having a fair complexion. I am sorry for having deceived you all these months.

Yours,

Sundri Devi.

Actress.'

ARTICLES

The third section of *Sone Chandi ke Buth* is a series of articles that are reflections on various aspects of cinema. From the business of films, emerging techniques and their impact, to the hierarchical structure strictly followed off screen and the celebration of films that have not succumbed to the commercial sensibilities of the marketplace, each article examines different facets of cinema as well as its impact on society.

The key article in this selection, as pointed out by Abbas in his Preface, is 'Living for Films, Dying for Films', which captures the experience of countless starstruck people, mesmerized by the glamour of films and propelled to make their way in the industry. Abbas offers practical advice to such people who need to showcase their talent through different avenues before taking the plunge and trying their luck in the film industry.

In 'Naye Film Naye Andaz', Abbas discusses film as being the 'most complex of all the fine arts' and contemplates the effect that technological advancements have on the medium. 'New Experiments in Indian Films' and 'Play of Light and

Shadows' take a critical look at commercial films, emphasizing the need for making films that reflect certain truths about life, while 'Film Industry: A Mirror of Our Society' discloses the casteist structure of the industry where each functionary has their place. In all of these articles, Abbas postulates the need for socially relevant films that concentrate on art, purpose, emotions, thoughts and ideas instead of those that chase glamour and sacrifice content in the process. He argues for the need for better scripts and emphasizes that, ultimately, a good story lies at the heart of a good film.

Film Industry: A Mirror of Our Society

Thousands of years ago, Manu divided Indian society into four categories or four castes. Just as by placing one earthen pot over another, one can construct a Qutub Minar made of mud, it was believed that God created this structure of the caste system where one caste was placed above another.

Right at the top of this minar were the Brahmins, followed by the Kshatriyas, then the Vaishyas and crushed below all of them were the Shudras. It is said that the castes were based on the division of labour. Those who could read and write ancient texts and perform religious rituals were called Brahmins. Kshatriyas were the arms-wielding brave soldiers and warriors. The traders and shopkeepers were the Vaishyas, and the Shudras were those who were forced to undertake the most menial and base jobs for the other three castes.

Exactly in the same way, film society is also divided into four categories.

The financier, who runs his business with the money of investors, dealers and businessmen, is at the top of this tower.

He charges an interest of 50–150 per cent on the money and that too in "black"! On the basis of the bills signed by the producer, one can put down any amount. The most interesting part is that the money is given after deducting the interest, which means that if someone has taken Rs 1 lakh on loan for one year and is to pay three times interest, the borrower will only receive Rs 68,000 while the receipt will be given for Rs 1 lakh. The amount of interest will be deducted from it beforehand and because it is certain that there will be a delay in returning the money, the producer's signatures will be taken on ten to twenty blank bills.

The next stratum is of people who borrow money from financiers in 'black' and pay the star of a film lakhs of rupees in 'black'. These people are known as producers but what they produce is not a film. Rather, they make a proposal for making a film. If A will be the hero, B the heroine and C and D the music directors, then the film can be sold for Rs 50 lakh. Distributors will then be ready to buy the film and financiers will also agree to give Rs 5–10 lakh to begin with. Hope springs eternal, and thus the entire film business is run on the basis of the proposal. Usually, the producer is someone who does not have money to invest in a film and even if he does, why would he risk his own money?

The money always comes in after the proposal, from either the financer or the distributor. This is the reason for placing the producer on a lower rung than the financier.

After them comes the film star. In a royal procession, there are usually two horsemen or two motorcyclists who escort the vehicle of the emperor or the king or that of a dictator and clear the way, and then the emperor's carriage arrives. Similarly, the film star is also placed on the third rung of this hierarchy. In reality, the position of the film star is probably higher than that of an emperor! That position is only reserved for the dictator. If, on a sunny day, a film star says it is night, the producer and director will promptly declare it to be night! And if the star says it's a bright, sunny day when it's actually night-time, then that would be agreed upon as well.

The film star could be the hero or the heroine; they both throw tantrums equally, but it is quite astonishing that, in fact, heroes throw far more tantrums than heroines. The heroes demand that shooting in the summer months should take place on air-conditioned sets. In the case of an outdoor shoot, the location should either be Shimla, Nainital, Mussoorie or Ooty, where the royal suite of a grand five-star hotel should be booked for their stay, and the hero can stay there along with his wife and kids or with his secretary and staff.

Those who have analysed this film society minutely have not been able to determine the status of the parents and grandparents of the heroine. There was a time when the heroine's maternal grandmother would tell the producer, 'Sethji, it has been many days now since our photograph has not appeared in the papers,' which meant that their Baby's photographs had not appeared in the media. However, this royal 'us' included both the grandmother and the heroine.

But these days, secretaries have replaced the grandmothers and mothers. The designation may have changed but the mannerisms remain much the same. There is a saying in the world of films, 'Today's secretary is tomorrow's producer,' which means, beware of every secretary. Who knows when one of them could become a producer?

You might be wondering why the film star has been placed on the third rung when they should be at the top of the ladder. This is the same as when the Vaishyas started thinking of themselves as more prominent than the Brahmins, or at least started hoping before it. The reality of today is that the foundation of society is not the study and knowledge of sacred texts but money, which neither the Brahmins nor the Kshatriyas possess. Only the businessmen have it who, according to the *Varnasrama,* are the Vaishyas and placed third in the hierarchy. In the same way, film stars are the richest and most powerful people in the industry. Accompanying them are a few music directors as well, who are no less than film stars, both in stature and mannerisms.

Despite being artists, the kind of wealth that stars possess will any day outweigh the wealth of businessmen. Although it is said that the stars are at the service of the producers, directors and financiers, in reality, producers, financiers and directors, all stand with folded hands in front of stars.

The fourth rung of this film society is comprised of the writers—the ones who write the story, screenplay, dialogue; cameramen, sound recordists, technicians, production manager, assistant director, etc. are all here. In the hierarchy of the film world, this constitutes the lowest rung, but it can easily be said that these people form the roots and foundation of this society.

Without them, no film can be made or exhibited, neither can it make any money. If one cameraman or his assistant makes a mistake of even 1 mm while fitting the lens in the camera, the hero, who is paid Rs 15 lakh, can be out of focus despite being in glorious technicolour! This holds true for the singer as well. They charge Rs 6000–7000 for a song but if the sound recordist or their assistant does not record the song properly, the singing can sound terrible! This is like our society—farmers who grow food grains, labourers who manufacture clothes or watches or cars in factories, or those who construct buildings, constitute the lowest rung despite being integral for its prosperity and development. They only earn a few rupees in lieu of their hard work while the sweat of their brow and their labour generates lakhs and crores of rupees for businessmen. Similarly, the hard-working people of film society languish in poverty despite being the very roots of this society.

Even though Shudras are placed lower than the other castes, there is differentiation among them too. Similarly, there is a hierarchy within the Shudras of the film society. The bottom-most rung among them belongs to the extras and coolies of the studios. These people only observe the glitz, glamour and riches of the film world from afar. Their own lives are devoid of any happiness as they are always short on funds and anxious about making ends meet. Their situation is similar to the majority of small farmers and labourers in the country.

So, effectively, this film society mirrors the society at large, as here too there is a similar hierarchy.

In both places, there is an abundance of money, happiness, air-conditioned hotels, big cars, but only for a few. This disparity is reflected in the film industry as well.

The veneer of glamour leads people to believe that the world of films is a unique one. But the reality is that here too, for a large section of the people who work hard and give the sweat of their brow, and sometimes even their blood for their work— the true artists and craftsmen—there is hunger, unemployment and lack of recognition. For a few lucky film stars, producers and a few financers, however, every comfort in the world is at their command.

I often think what would happen if revolution came to the film society. Will the situation not be like it is in other countries?

Till when will we continue to be placed one on top of the other like the Qutub Minar made out of earthen pots?

It will take just one earthquake, one storm to make these earthen pots come crashing to the ground. Even if inequality is not completely eradicated, it will be diminished to a large extent.

Certain films that are now being made focus on art, purpose, emotions, thoughts and ideas.

Instead of featuring expensive film stars, these films feature good actors. The success of one such film will not change the financial fortune of anyone, but they are being appreciated by the masses to some extent.

At last, if not a complete revolution, then at least a significant change has been brought about in film society, just like a significant change has been brought about in our larger society. We all need to remember that film society is a part of this world and exemplifies our larger society.

Play of Light and Shadows

Lights on.
Lights off.
Turn on the lights.
Turn off the lights.
Light.
Dark again.
Again light.
And then darkness.

The whole business of films is the play of light and shadows, whether the film is in black and white or in colour.

These days, every film is made in colour and is framed in ways that captures patterns and the effects made by the interplay between darkness and light.

It is integral for films to evoke the opposing emotions of happiness and sadness. It is especially essential that Indian films and those from South Asia have elements of comedy, tragedy, romance and action. It is important they have a hero and a villain, a heroine and a vamp, and songs, laughter and tears. Here, a successful film gains immense prominence because we don't have much theatre or opera, or music and dance halls. Instead, we depend on cinema for everything. This is why people have become accustomed to watching films that bring so many elements together—an emotional story, social issues, comedy, action, songs and dance sequences.

But, at this point, I am talking about illumination and darkness from a creative standpoint, a qualitative standard. Good films illuminate the hearts and minds of people while bad films infuse them with gloom.

Seen from this perspective, cinema is a play of shadows and light. Our standards of what constitutes a good film keeps varying, in keeping with our assessment of films from other nations. At one time, American films were very popular and at another, Russian or French films, followed by Italian films. After the era of Polish films, it was the turn of Japanese films and now the whole world seems fond of Czechoslovakian films. Similarly, in Indian films too, we sometimes see the light of high artistry, and sometimes the darkness of bad taste and flat comedy. From this perspective, the current era of Hindi films is one of darkness. At one point we used to make serious, meaningful and artistic films like *Devdas* (1935), *Duniya Na Mane* (1937) and *Aadmi* (1939), and then we started making nonsensical films like *Khazanchi* (1958), *Khidki* (1948) and *Shin Shinaki Boobla Boo* (1952). Then, once again, Indian cinema took a turn and we saw films of a certain calibre, like *Pather Panchali* (1955), *Do Bigha Zamin* (1953), *Awara* (1951), *Boot Polish* (1954), *Mirza Ghalib* (1954) and *Munna* (1954). Then came the era of colour films and, dazzled by the brilliance of colours, we abandoned art, intent, performance and the interplay of characters.

The use of colour in some films is so heavy-handed that it sometimes feels like a box of crayons was handed over to a child who randomly splashed the colours on a white canvas. It is expensive to make colour films. It costs about Rs 2 lakh to shoot a black-and-white film and make fifty copies of it, whereas it costs Rs 10 lakh for the same for colour films! This is why those who make colour films are afraid to experiment. Huge sums of money are paid to famous film stars to star in colour films, expensive music directors are called upon for the songs and music, and grand, costly sets are constructed. A lot of money is spent on dancers, costumes and elaborate decorations and in this way, the budget of a colour film easily reaches Rs 30-50 lakh and goes up to Rs 60–70 lakh.

It is easy to make a colour film or rather it once was. The formula for success consists of popular film stars, a prominent music director, dances, grand sets, gaudy dresses and expensive embellishments. Distributors quickly snap up the film or, rather, they once did. Theatre owners excitedly screen these films, or rather they did at one point. Regular filmgoers also enjoy these films or rather they did so in the past. In this comparison between the past and the present reality lies the entire story of Indian cinema and, much like ordinary Indian films, this story too includes both comic and tragic elements.

The Indian film market is divided into six territories— Delhi and Uttar Pradesh constitute one territory; Bengal, Assam, Orissa and Bihar come in the second; central India, that includes Rajasthan and Madhya Pradesh, constitutes the third territory; the southern states, including Andhra Pradesh, Tamil Nadu, Mysore, Kerala, form the fourth; Punjab is the fifth; and overseas forms the sixth territory. During the heyday of colour films, a film with big stars would be sold for Rs 7–12 lakh but that could in no way determine its success at the box office or its ability to earn a profit. That would depend on the mood of the audience, the kind of films they preferred and their spending power. Most of the films that were released in 1967 were colour films which failed at the box office. Neither the popularity of the film stars worked nor the use of exuberant colour. Elaborate dance sequences, songs, grand sets and scenes shot in exotic locations like Switzerland and Kashmir all failed to impress the audiences. Distributors suffered huge losses and caused an uproar. The central India territory decided that they wouldn't pay more than Rs 6.5 lakh even for films with the biggest stars and that too on an advance, which meant that producers would have to compensate for losses. Following suit, the distributors from other territories also decided to do the same. Overnight, the price of films was reduced to half! Given this situation, where could the producers look to cut costs and increase their revenues?

Most of the revenue earned from films goes to the government in the form of entertainment tax. Then theatre owners take a large share. There is only a small amount that comes to the distributor and producer. In fact, sometimes they need to put in money from their own pockets to pay for the theatres. Such was the situation in the past. So, to cut down on their expenses, the producers convinced theatre owners of Bombay not to charge them for the hiring of theatres, and instead to come aboard as partners, taking a percentage from the revenue earned by the films.

The current circumstances are both meaningful and meaningless, and include elements of comedy and tragedy. After a month-long dispute, the theatres in Bombay have now reopened but the studios still remain shut.[1] Producers are continuing to wage a war on four fronts—against the entertainment tax; against distributors so that they do not reduce the costs of films and not insist on the advance; against the exhibitors so they reduce their charges; and also against the stars of the films so that they too lower their fee. In fact, this fight has now become a five-fronted one because there is discord among the producers themselves, wherein the big producers are on one side and the small producers on the other.

One member described what was happening, 'There is discord between them regarding the division of profits. This is the result of the deeds of the producers, which has reached its zenith, and now they are baffled at the situation, unable to decide what they should do.'

In such an atmosphere, who can think about the artistic excellence of cinema? Film producers themselves say that filmmaking is a business, an industry and a trade but this

---

[1] The reference is to the shutdown of theatres that took play in Bombay in 1968. There were a series of conflicts that took place between 1967–1968 within the film industry. Due to several reasons, film producers, exhibitors and distributors waged a war with each other during this time. As Abbas points out, the shift to colour films and exotic locations entailed high production costs which correspondingly meant high losses when the film failed at the box office. There were several intertwined issues that were plaguing the industry at the time that exacerbated the problems; in January 1968, distributors in north India demanded advance payment from producers. This had a ripple effect and producers put forth their own set of demands. As the problems escalated, cinemas shut down and finally reopened on 24 March 1968 after being shut for nineteen days. However, film production did not resume as there were several issues within the production sector that were yet to be addressed at the time. The production ban was finally lifted in May 1968.

industry is unique. It can make crores of people laugh and cry. Sometimes it even compels them to think, which is why, despite being a business, it is an art, an exceptional art, a very dangerous art, which can widen the good taste of the public or make them regress, eroding their values and civility.

There are a few crazy people who, despite the emphasis on commerce, are thinking about artistic excellence and issue-based films, and are trying to make films that may or may not be commercially successful. They are meaningful, progressive, artistically beautiful and pure. Art still blooms even amid the dry and gloomy world of business. For example, in 1966, when films with a budget of Rs 50–60 lakh, made with a firm eye on profit and which included the requisite songs and dance numbers and all the other components, started failing miserably, Chetan Anand made a small black-and-white film, *Aakhri Khat* (1966). The film did not have any big star. The hero was a one-and-a-half-year-old child, but the film was artistic and heart-warming. It was widely appreciated and, in some places, even fared better than many colour films starring big stars. Prior to this, there was a film made by Shailendra in a similar vein, *Teesri Kasam* (1966). It was a simple but meaningful story of ordinary rural folk, based on a popular Hindi novel. It was awarded the President's Gold Medal for Best Feature Film. Sadly, keeping commercial sensibilities in mind, there were so many modifications made in the film that despite receiving such a prestigious award, it could not be released in several places. It could not even be released in Bombay, where the film was made! This is the most apt example of the tussle between art and commerce.

Sometimes, a few crazy people, who are well aware of the commercial aspect of films, can adapt a fine, purposeful story and make a film which fuses its objective, meaning, art and commerce to create a worthy confluence. Such films are unique and the artistic element is comparably weak. Raj Kapoor's *Sangam* (1964) was such a film—a good, emotional story, with effective dialogues, fine performances, superior techniques, all topped with famous songs, dance sequences, fantastic settings and beautiful scenes shot abroad, all of which created such a dazzling effect that the film found astounding success. Another example is Manoj Kumar's film *Upkar* (1967). The secret to this film's success lies in its impressive story, appropriate dialogues and feelings of patriotism that were brought together with little melodrama and crude emotions. But such films are only made once in a while.

The current situation has producers worried. They are tense and flustered. They want to make films with smaller budgets. A few among them want to make meaningful films but fewer still have the courage to face the truth. The truth is that despite the presence of expensive stars and music directors who are paid in lakhs, the inclusion of ten to twelve songs, group dances with fifty girls, beautiful locales of Switzerland and Kashmir, films are failing to succeed. Bunching together these diverse components or the presence of any one of them will not make a film successful. Isn't it high time, then, that instead of chasing big stars and music directors, producers should start focusing on the story? The story should be engaging and meaningful, one that mirrors the life of the people and is presented in an appealing manner. Now that expensive formulas are failing, why not try out this cheap formula? Perhaps here may lie the salvation of the silver screen!

Naye Film Naye Andaz

Thank god. Films are now included as fine arts. So far, they had been considered no better than substandard nautanki. Frankly, though, some films remind one of nautanki.

They say films have all the elements of the fine arts: literature, poetry, music, painting, sculpture. If films are made as a business and not an art, their sole purpose is to make quick money.

Cinema is a combined effort of many artists; it aggregates as an independent artistic medium. It has its own rules, own grammar, own narrative style. Its uniqueness lies in its expansiveness, like the ocean. There is nothing outside its reach, whether in this world or in outer space. But it requires complex mechanical devices to achieve the depth, the expanse, the allurement. In addition to artists, therefore, it needs expert technicians and, of course, lots of money.

Writers of greatest classics of the past needed a brain and imagination besides reams of paper. Or a typewriter, a fountain pen, a quill pen with a pot of ink, even the humble pencil.

The world's best music needs the human voice or a Re 1 flute made of simple bamboo reed which can play the sweetest melodies.

For film you need camera, raw stock, a cameraperson, sound, laboratory, an editor, an editing room. Studio shooting requires light, sets, the combined labour of a few hundred people, their labour, skill, dedication and, of course, pots of money. Only then is a film made.

This is the most complex of all the fine arts. And the most expensive. It requires many artists and precise equipment working in synergy. Many times, its artistic aspect is ignored because of its commercial and technical aspects. The words 'That one is a jubilee hit' mean a running period of twenty-five weeks and a box office collection of multiple lakhs. Or you may hear, 'Grand, spectacular sets' or 'Songs will be sure hits'. Rarely does one hear the beauty of the message or the importance of the subject.

A French director said, 'Film will become art when the stock will cost the same as paper and when camera can be as easily bought as a film reel.'

An argument was going on at an international film festival: What Is Film—Art or Technique?

A big Indian director said, 'The speed at which new techniques are being developed in cinema . . . a revolution is on the horizon.'

An English director said, 'Colour film has changed not only its photography but the director's orientation.'

A French film critic said, 'Cinemascope and 70mm has not only expanded the film screen but expanded the imagination of the art of film-making.'

At that moment, a famous Indian film writer took a fountain pen out of his pocket. 'Look at my pen. It costs Rs 150. It has a gold tip and its ink is vacuum-filled. Its makers claim it is the best pen the world over.'

Those present were thinking if he was part of the discussion or if he was advertising his pen. The writer continued his speech. 'Kalidas wrote his classics on Bhoj Patra with the edge of a broken bird wing. Ghalib wrote his ghazals with a quill made from bamboo. Munshi Premchand wrote with a one-anna holder pen which constantly had to be dipped in the pot of ink. And me? I write with this vacuumatic gold-tipped pen. My late friend Saadat Hasan Manto wrote with two fingers on an old typewriter. In the US not only novelists and essayists, even scenario writers and poets write their pieces on electric typewriters. The progress of writing technique is phenomenal.

'But can anyone say that my vacuumatically written screenplay will reach greater heights than Prem Chand's holder pen-written short stories? Can it be said that poetry has reached great heights today compared to its stature in the works of Kalidas, Ghalib, Shakespeare or Goethe? Because what we compose in this atomic age is written on an advanced instrument?

'Art and literature are created from the depths of human imagination not through some state of art instruments. All instruments are merely that; camera, projector, typewriter, photo copier, all are simply means of transmitting the imagination and vision of the artist to the world.'

At this point, the argument at the colloquium ended, but world over, film people endlessly argued about the impact of new techniques and inventions on film-making.

There is no doubt whatsoever that art is created by human genius, not mechanical genius. Equipment of any kind or quality serve to transmit the imagination of the artist to the *awam*.

The camera is the director's brush and pen. It brings expression to the director's vision. Wielding it is simple; even a child can do it. Complexity lies in making the film. It's not simply capturing the scene the director wants. The combination of the lens number, the aperture, the light and shade balance, all of that counts.

Compared to all the arts, technique is very important in film. New techniques have to be deployed for optimum results.

Twin revolutions are happening across the world in film technique. They are parallel but also convergent.

Competition with television has led to new gimmicks across the world. First appeared colour films, then cinemascope, then Cinerama which created the illusion of an expanse as far as the human eye could see. After being silent for a while, thirty-five years ago, films got a voice. Now voice has got new technical inputs. Film arts and artists have been gainers. Film stars who could not hold a single note are singing beautifully. A new reality dawned with colour films. Life is not all black and white. Commercial considerations used colour to stun the audience; it never claimed to bring reality closer. Colour sets became so removed from reality that votaries of realism became disgusted with colour. They continued with black and white although colour, if used with truth and moderation, can imbue the film with unique realism. Sound began its new avatar. Stereophonic, melody-mix, fusion created new syntheses. TV was born of the blend of techniques of film and radio. The two are a love-hate duo but partners, regardless. They have a deep, mutual impact, no doubt.

While on the one hand, competition from TV created cinemascope and hugely expensive films, it was also instrumental in bringing cinema back towards realism. TV film is cheaper than feature film, a factor which led to a new phenomenon. While on the one hand, massive films with mega budgets were being made with the sole objective of dazzling the audience, on the other, another reality began to emerge. Small film-makers, inspired by TV, began a quest for 'lived life' and its truth which they chased with their shoulder cameras and portable sound equipment—cheap cameras with internal sound, 'fast' reel which works in semi-darkness, low-cost, almost weightless, lights, equipment which can be carried anywhere. Young film-makers who have moved from the hothouse of commercial *mahaul* of films are thereby capturing reality through *qalambund* (pen) or *filmbund* (reel).

The future of cinema and new techniques is linked to this new urge. The urge which is neither to worship technology as a deity nor be in its awe of this 'new monster'. It is, rather, utilizing its every aspect to sketch for viewers, life, its reality and its truth.

Living for Films, Dying for Films

The doorbell sounds; it is loud and persistent, as if announcing, 'I am here. The one you were waiting for. Open the door. This door and all doors of life—because if you don't open, I have the muscle to break it open. This door and every door of life; all doors which will come in my way.'

I quickly open the door.

A young man is standing and a taxi is waiting outside. Its meter is ticking away. I take stock. The hair is styled like Dilip Kumar but the smell is of cheap oil. New shave, a jet-like thin moustache, a bright floral shirt, pink sharkskin pants and two-toned pointed shoes.

'What can I do for you?' I ask, beckoning him towards a chair.

'I have brought a letter from your old classmate Mr Sharma, the lawyer from Meerut. He is my father's close friend.'

The letter says this young man has come to Bombay to look for employment, and to help him.

'What do you want to do?' I ask.

'I want to work in films.'

'What kind of work?'

'As a hero!'

'Have you acted in stage plays?'

'No. But my friends say I look like a hero.'

'Have you worked in radio plays?'

'No.'

'Then what makes you say that you want to work in films?'

'I know I can. All I need is your recommendation. You just need to introduce me to the right people.'

I did not have time to argue with or explain anything to this young man. Thousands of such youth (matric fail, matric pass, Inter, BA, MA) hang around the studios in Bombay. I hand him two–three recommendation letters. I know it will not be of much use because I have written hundreds of such letters which are still doing the rounds of various studios.

Five weeks later, the doorbell rings again. But it does not sound like it did the first time. This time it sounds like it's thinking… it is hesitating… as if it is apologizing for disturbing me, as if it is saying, 'If you don't mind, please open the door.'

I put down my newspaper slowly and get up. And then leisurely walk to the door. The same young man is there but behind him, on the road, I don't see a taxi. The red bus of Bombay Corporation is disappearing in a cloud of dust. The young man's hair is combed back with water, not oil. There is two or three days of growth on his chin, his jet-like moustache appears as if the jet engine has failed and crashed to the ground. His colourful bush shirt has lost its colour from frequent washing and has not been ironed. His pink sharkskin trousers have become dirty. His pointed shoes have not been polished for many days, and their soles are completely worn out.

'So how are you now?' I ask the question, though the answer is evident before my eyes.

'Sir, I am okay . . . Some people have promised to give me work . . . one film will start next week . . . they have promised . . .'

'Promised to give you the role of a hero?'

'Not a hero, Sir, a side role has been promised.'

'That's good news.'

'Yes, sir. But there is a delay in starting the film. Financing has still not been arranged. Till then . . . if you can give me a loan of Rs 50. I will return it as soon as the film starts.'

I give him Rs 5 and see him to the door.

Five months later, the bell rings again. Did I say ring? A soft, barely audible 'tring', that's all. As if someone hesitatingly touched the bell and quickly removed the finger. This time I can hardly recognize the youth. This is not the same face, his eyes have sunk. Around them are dark circles. He hasn't shaved for days, his hair is tangled and dry and has not seen scissors for months. His lips are chapped, his shoes are covered in dust and worn out. The bright floral bush shirt cannot be seen beneath the dirt, those sharkskin trousers which used to be pink have become grey with dirt and are torn at the knee.

'Please get me some water, I have walked all the way from the station,' he says as he flops down. I ask my servant to get a cup of tea. I want to ask him, 'So . . . how are you?' But the question does not rise to my lips. With trembling hands, he drinks the tea as if he has been hungry for days.

I watch him quietly.

After finishing the tea, he says, 'Sometimes I get work as an extra . . . But for a few weeks now, the industry has been dead . . . No shooting is going on in any studio.'

'Where are you staying?'

'In Dadar, Sir. Main road, Ranjit Studio. I have left my
bedding in a paan shop . . . that is where I sleep.'

And now I say what I should have said five months ago:
'You are suffering so much, why don't you go back home?' He
thinks a little and then slowly stands up.

'How will I go home, Sir? Now I have to live and I have to
die . . . in this film world.'

This is not a made-up story, this is a true incident. This
young man's name is Ram Krishan; it is also Mohammed Anwar;
it is also Daljeet Singh. There are thousands of such young men
who come from all over the country. From Lucknow, from
Ludhiana, from Bangalore, from Benaras, from Cochin, from
Kanpur. They keep coming, coming and coming. Among them
are university and college graduates, there are matric fail, there
are semi-literates. They are children of rich elite, they are the
hope of poor households. They are those who take thousands
of rupees from their parents and arrive here to conquer the
Great Bombay Film World. They are those who travel all the
way from their village to Bombay without a railway ticket. I
used to know a young *jagirdar* who, when he came to Bombay,
had a car worth Rs 8000. The car was so unique, so sleek that
people used to crowd at Marine Drive to catch a glimpse of
it. Today he borrows money from friends, so he can travel in
public buses and do the rounds of Bombay film studios.

A few of them come with the hope of becoming directors,
story-writers or dialogue-writers, but most of them dream
of becoming top film stars like Dilip Kumar or Raj Kapoor.
Dreamers, all of them indefatigable dreamers. Many of them
spend a few weeks or a few months wandering from studio to
studio and then . . . go back home. Hundreds of them join the
line-up of extras and live in the hope that one day some sharp-

eyed producer-director will glance their way and the miracle will happen! They have heard that every year, out of thousands of aspirants, there are one or two, who, because of their hard work, their talent, or even kismet, taste success! In this hope, thousands of 'man chale' and 'sar phire' leave their homes and buy tickets to Bombay. This has been going on for the last fifty years and who knows how long it will continue!

Why has this happened?

Is this normal? Is this inevitable? Is there no cure for this mental fixation?

My first question is why. There is no simple answer. Our youth sees dazzling glamour in film life. Cars, flats, huge contracts—all these ephemeral dreams stun their senses. They are trapped in this golden web and lose their rational mind. With closed eyes, they start supplicating before the film wallahs. It is obvious that it is not an untreatable disease; the youth who want to enter the film world and rise to the top should be shown the right way. They should be given guidance and appropriate opportunities. In other countries, there are highly reputed film institutions where aspiring actors can seek training. Only after this rigorous drilling do they take the final step. Unfortunately, in our country, such institutions don't exist. But there is the stage, there is the radio and literature, and those who succeed on those platforms, those are the ones that film wallahs are always looking for.

As for the youth who want to enter the film world, as story writers, dialogue-writers or lyricists, I have a suggestion. Before even thinking of films, they should make their place in literature—write a novel, write a story, write a poem, write a *geet*. Whenever someone comes to me with a stack of manuscripts, I ask him one question, 'If a publisher is not even prepared to spend a few thousands to publish your stories, then how can a director risk lakhs of rupees for them?'

In short, I tell them, 'If you think you are a great artist, act in a play and give me proof of your talent.

'You think you can write screenplay or dialogues? Then write a great novel or a dozen stories so that you first become famous across this country.

'You think you are a better singer than Mukesh or Rafi or you think you are a better singer than Lata, then use the medium of radio and gramophone to prove your talent. If you do that, the film wallahs will themselves seek you out.'

New Experiments in Indian Films

These days there is a lot of talk about 'new wave cinema'. But to tell you the truth, experiments have always been conducted in Indian cinema.

The first experiment was by Dadasaheb Phalke in his film *Raja Harishchandra*. Then, Debaki Bose made *Seeta* and *Rajrani Meera*. P.C. Barua's films—*Devdas, Maya* and *Manzil*—were made in the same genre. In those days, the usual *chalu* films like *Toofan Mail* were being made. Then V. Shantaram made *Duniya Na Mane, Aadmi* and *Padosi*. They were not just an experiment, they were a revolution in the Bombay film industry. When I made *Dharti ke Lal* and Chetan Anand made *Neecha Nagar*, we did not stop to think that it was an experiment. The direction of Indian cinema had turned towards films like *Duniya na Mane* and *Devdas*. These were serious films in which the stories were about real, not reel, life.

Whether it's music or art, literature or poetry, there are two ways of evaluating them. First, what is the writer or poet trying to say, and second, how is he saying it? This is the crux of form and content: the age-old argument whether form is more important or content? This discourse has been going on in India for 2000 years! I believe that real art is that which fulfils the requirement of Satyam Shivam Sundaram. Satyam is truth, social and psychological, that is number one. Second is Sundaram, which means beauty. Some films reflect the truth, social and psychological, and present it as it is, in its stark form. Other films are more about technique, less about content—the emphasis is flipped. I must add here that, after a long time, the importance of these experimental films with 'different' storywriters has been recognized.

In our society, as the glamour of colour films is increasing, the worth of stars is becoming phenomenal. Technique, especially photography, is in high demand, and the value of story and storywriters is decreasing. There was a time when producers used to say with great pride that this is Sarat Chandra Chatterjee's story, this is Rabindranath Tagore's book, this film is based on Premchand's novel. But over time, in Hindi films, all these great writers were forgotten. Now in the credits we see the line, 'This story comes from our own Story Department.'

Instead of a solid story, screenplay and formulas have taken over. It is the Hollywood formula—boy meets girl!

One boy, one girl

One boy, two girls

Two boys, one girl

Neither the boy nor the girl belong to this earth.

The boy and girl meet; they look at each other and immediately fall in love. They sing four songs, two duets, one dance, the heroine dances, the hero beats the drums, the villain spoils the scene, misunderstandings occur, the hero sings a sad song, the heroine sings a sad song. Climax. There is a fist fight, the villain falls down from a mountain and the hero and heroine are reunited.

It is not easy to compete with such commercial, chalu films. Especially those where Rs 20 or 30 lakh have been invested in these star-studded productions. But there are some mad young people who think of art films even in this highly commercial world. Regardless of their success at the box office, they leave a deep impression on the hearts and minds of the audience. Film business is like gambling or lottery. No one can say which film would be successful or why it would be successful. That is why sometimes, by mistake, even films with a serious and solid story become big hits.

My film *Shehar aur Sapna* was refused by forty distributors because it had no songs, no dance sequences, no cabarets, no glamorous sets, no stars. The hero and heroine were plain-looking. But when it got the President's Gold Medal, it became a hit. A small film with a small budget became a moderate box office hit!

In 1966, when commercial films worth Rs 50–60 lakh were failing at the box office, Chetan Anand made a small black-and-white film called *Aakhri Khat*. It had no famous or successful star; its real hero was a two-year-old boy. But it was imbued with so much beauty and emotion that it became a hit. In some regions, it fared better than many expensive star-studded films.

In the same manner, a simple but impressive film was made by Shailendra and directed by a young Bengali, Basu Bhattacharya. It was called *Teesri Kasam*. Despite the fact that it had stars like Raj Kapoor and Waheeda Rehman, the film was special because it showed the ordinary life of village folk. It was based on a story of the famous writer Phanishwar Nath Renu.

These three films became the talk of the town. *Teesri Kasam* also got the President's Gold Medal.

There was one commonality in these three films—the story. Each story could be called a true reflection of our society. After many years, due to the teamwork of Sarat Chandra Chatterjee and Barua, the time had come when films were becoming successful because of their stories. Their success proved the fact that if the story is interesting, if it has a message and if it is close to life, it can be successful even without top stars and music directors.

It is unfortunate that the success of these films has not shaken the commercial film world. The time has come when producers should explore the stories of visionary writers and stop running after big stars and music directors.

In recent times, the National Film Finance Corporation has decided to support only films that have good storylines. They will finance films that have a new element, a new style, a new narration. In addition to that, writers in various languages have started taking greater interest in films. As a result, the value of writers has increased in all Indian films, especially Hindi films.

The famous Malyalam novelist Thakazhi Suvasankara Pillai wrote a novel called *Chemmeen*; a beautiful film was made on it by director Ramu Kariat. It became known all over India because that year, *Chemmeen* got the President's Gold Medal. In the same way, the famous Kannada novel *Samskara* was made into a film by director Pattabhirama Reddy and dramatist Girish Karnad. The film was very powerful, and it also got the President's Gold Medal.

It was Rajinder Singh Bedi who made a deep impact on the Hindi film industry. He made a film based on his own famous play *Naql-e-Makani*. He wrote the screenplay for the film *Dastak,* and also directed and produced it. The film was gripping, it had philosophical depth, it had psychological insight and it was sharply critical of society. It was presented in an entirely new manner. Bedi is one of the top writers of Urdu, but so far, he has written screenplays and dialogues of formula films. He was the writer, director and producer of *Dastak,* that is why he could say all he wanted in his very special, sharp, incisive style.

During this time, Basu Chatterjee made *Sara Aakash.* Its story was written by a well-known Hindi writer Rajendra Yadav. He wrote about middle-class life in his native Agra. The beauty of the story was that it did not appear like 'a story'. It seemed like a simple incident in the life of a small, humble family. The film was shot in Agra, in the very house around which Rajendra Yadav had written his story. Basu Chatterjee used some technical stunts to show the Agra samaj, but the story remained detached from formula and close to real life.

Famous Bengali director Mrinal Sen used a short story by Banaphool for a film called *Bhuvan Shome.* It was beautifully filmed in Hindi and its camerawork was exceptional. To some extent, it was successful at the box office and received the President's Gold Medal. Its basic structure, however, was very different from that of formula films. Its success was proof of the fact that our viewers are ready to see films that reject formula; in fact, they are very interested in such films.

This film *Badnam Basti* presented a fine novelist and storywriter, Kamleshwar, before the film world. It is based on *Badnaam Gali,* and was the work of a young director, Prem Kapoor. But it could not achieve the heights that this deeply thoughtful story deserved. The reason for this could be that Prem Kapoor had not yet mastered the technique which was used by experts in such films. When we make experimental films, there is a possibility that they might not succeed. The important thing is that the old formulas were rejected and an experiment was carried out.

Mani Kaul has made a film called *Uski Roti*, which is based on Mohan Rakesh's story. It has not yet been released, so I cannot say how many people will understand this highly complex film. It's about a simple married woman from a village in Punjab. The presentation of the woman is stark and complex. At the same time, it is a new experiment. Would our filmmakers and film viewers be able to understand intricacies of the human mind which the film has tried to depict?

Anubhav is also an experiment, in which director Basu Bhattacharya has presented the relationship between a married couple and given a new answer to an old question.

Today, many new films are in the process of being made or have been completed and are awaiting release. In all these stories, some dark corner of the labyrinth called life has been illuminated. These include Mohan Rakesh's drama *Aadhe Adhure*, which has been a stage success. Another play by Mohan Rakesh, which is even deeper and more symbolic, is *Ashadh Ka Ek Din,* which Mani Kaul has filmed with an entirely new technique. There is Kamleshwar's story *Phir Bhi*, which has been directed by Shivendra Sinha and has been awarded the National Film Award for best feature film in Hindi.

Subodh Ghosh's Bengali story *Ek Adhuri Kahani* has been produced by Arun Kaul and directed by Mrinal Sen.

New kind of stories, new kind of films, new experiments.
In Hindi
In Malayalam.
In Bengali.

In Kannada.

It is possible that such experiments will be made in other languages too. This is an auspicious moment in our cinema when some Indian films have been freed from the golden shackles of formula films!

But the treasury of stories has not been exhausted yet. So far, only a few Hindi writers' stories have been filmed. We still have several novels, and many stories of Premchand waiting to be filmed. So far, no one has dared touch Sarat Chandra Chatterjee's classic *Srikanta*. Rajinder Singh Bedi, Krishan Chander, Ismat Chughtai, Balwant Singh, Ram Lal, Amrita Pritam—so many acutely thoughtful and gripping stories written by them are waiting to be shown on the silver screen.

Experimentation in Hindi cinema has only just begun.

BOMBAY CHRONICLE
ARTICLES

As the political correspondent and later film critic for the *Bombay Chronicle,* Khwaja Ahmad Abbas began his foray in film journalism in the 1930s. With full freedom to be as critical as he wanted to be, Abbas embarked on his job as a film critic with gusto, watching some 300 Indian and foreign films in a year. He received brickbats for some of his reviews and the threat of film advertising being withdrawn from the *Chronicle.* However, he was not deterred from his responsibility as a film critic—that of informing audiences correctly about a film, so that they may decide whether or not they would watch it. He was invited by Baburao Patel to contribute articles to *Filmindia,* once again, without any constraints.

In this section of the book, we present a few film reviews by Abbas, which provide an insight into the journalistic style at the time. Abbas did not mince his words, showering unabashed praise on the films that he felt were worthy and soundly dismissing the ones that were not, pointing out their many faults but also pointing out their redeeming features, if he could find any!

The reviews are followed by his editorial pieces on cinema and the art of film criticism. At a time when the call for the independence of India was gaining momentum, he contemplates the medium of cinema and its ability to communicate ideas, and the ways in which films contribute towards spearheading a national language.

In the insightful 'From "Harishchandra" to "Adhikar": Quarter Century of Indian Films', he offers a historical overview of the film industry, taking us through the transformations over the decades, while in 'When Death Stalks the Studios' he raises the crucial question of the insurance of studio employees and their safety. Several issues raised in these articles prompt us to reflect the current state of films in our country and wonder how much has really changed over the decades.

'Durga'—Portrait of a Village!

Bombay Talkies New Film at Roxy, Devaki Rani Returns to the Screen
July 1939

Inimitable Devika Rani returned to the screen at Roxy on Saturday, after almost a whole year, much to the delight of her numerous fans. She appeared in (and as) 'Durga', Bombay Talkies' latest production.

But the most important thing in *Durga* is not Devika Rani, though she plays the title role with her usual vivacity and verve, putting out a brilliant, well-rounded performance. It is not Rama Shukul (who acts with quiet competence in a role hopelessly subdued) and it is not Mumtaz Ali who, as Pagla, seems to have suddenly acquired a marvellous voice. It is not even the generally excellent technique.

It is the hard manual labour that she has to do to eke out a living for herself and her daughter. Overwork causes a heart-attack and while the widow lies dying, Durga has to look about for a doctor. But she has only two annas to pay the fee—'That is what my mother got for grinding corn yesterday,' she says! Two annas for a whole day's work! Two annas a day for a mother and a daughter and a goat to live on! However, much film producers wish to keep away from such uncomfortable things, economic realities have a way of intruding in the most unsuspecting ways. The death of Durga's mother epitomizes the problem of rural poverty in India. The uncomfortable feeling persists that she might have been saved if only she had been getting a decent living wage.

Young Doctor Jawahar

Her mother dead, Durga is thrown back on her own resources and naturally becomes self-assertive and daring. She has two friends—Pagla, the mad mendicant, and Jawahar, the young doctor. Pagla is, of course, the latest edition of the philosophic blind singer and his female counterpart had already made an appearance in Bombay Talkies' *Janma Bhoomi* (*Dunya kehli mujh ko pagal, main kehti dunya ko pagal!*). Dr Jawahar is an interesting type—modern, young India. He has dedicated his life to the service of the village but (in contrast with the hero of *Janma Bhoomi*) he has not become a Brahmachari. He laughs and loves, as well as gives injections and is more of a human being than the usual idealist of the films. His lighter moments with Durga are delightful and the nobility of character implicit in his treatment of his rival, the compounder Meghraj, is exemplary. But on the whole this character is too soft and goody-goody to be effective in comparison with the dynamic personality of Durga.

Shadow of the Sahukar

And thus, loved by Pagla and Jawahar and hated by the entire village she continued to live in the village until a new factor appeared in her life in the person of Sahukar Makhan. It is impossible to imagine a village moneylender and not be faced with the terrible economic system he represents. He is as much a part of the rural life in India as malaria or malnutrition. Like a conqueror he rides into the village on a palanquin and holds court. He is a bloodsucker, of course, but he is sweet of tongue and, as he repeatedly declares, keeps strictly within the law. The worse for the law!

Unscrupulous as he is, he entices the naïve and unsophisticated Durga, whose hut has been burnt and who is now homeless, to go and live with him—hoping ultimately to persuade her to marry him. Incredible as it may seem the wily Sahukar turns out to be not so bad after all, and under the influence of Durga he turns over a new leaf—and once again an Indian film sidetracks the indictment of the Sahukari system. So good, indeed, the Sahukar becomes that he foregoes his claims on a debtor, treats Durga like a daughter and even helps her to marry Jawahar, whom she has all along loved.

Tame Ending

The Sahukar is thus reformed but Durga is spoilt—presumably by the comfortable life in the Sahukar's house. She loses all that fire and daring which were her dominant traits. The girl who had once defiantly told Jawahar she would marry him now becomes so subdued that when she hears he is marrying someone else simply collapses and remains lying in the same position for hours on end while the Sahukar goes to fetch Jawahar. The doctor himself (very callously and irrationally) gives away his would-be bride (as if she were a sack of potatoes) to an obliging friend and comes running to Durga. The story which had elements of strong drama becomes tame and insipid in the end, which is very unfortunate.

It is equally unfortunate that the dialogues and the words of the songs failed to do justice to what was essentially a powerful and original story. Even though the treatment tended towards the conventional. (Even the good old duet-and-dance-in drama sequence appeared!)

Devika Puts Life in 'Durga'

Devika Rani, however, makes ample amends for any such minor lapses in the film. She makes Durga live on the screen and once again she proves herself to be the leading dramatic actress in India.

Next to her, the most outstanding performance is that of Aundhkar as the Sahukar. Shukul manfully strives to do justice to rather a subsidiary role. Mumtas is as good as Pagla (who did not turn out to be so mad after all) while V.H. Desai proves many a laugh by his subtle clowning.

If anyone asked me for a film picturing India's village life, I would recommend *Durga*. If anyone wanted to see first rate acting, I would ask him to see Devika Rani in *Durga*.

'The Mill'—But What About 'Mazdoor'?

Ajanta Film Shown at Imperial After Years of Censors' Ban
14 June 1939

Five years ago, I still remember, the production of *The Mill* (alias 'Mazdoor') created sensation after sensation.

The announcement that Munshi Premchand was to write the story was by itself news of first-rate importance. It was for the first time that a producer in Western India had availed of the services of such an eminent literary personality.

Mr Bhavnani, who had founded Ajanta Movietone, was reputed to be an educated and progressive director-producer, and one expected him to turn out a film of a really high quality.

The theme—Labour versus Capital—was not entirely new. I had seen it treated, albeit crudely, in an earlier production *Wrath* (the original title, 'The Bomb', having been banned by the censors) but one expected a more straightforward and vigorous treatment from the new team of Bhavnani and Premchand.

Banned!

And, then, one day *The Mill* struck the headlines by being banned by the censors.

It is difficult to remember the exact sequence of events but, I believe, the film was revised, shown again to the censors, banned for the second time, and ultimately allowed to be shown in some other provinces. But the results are well-known—Munshi Premchand retired from scenario writing and later died without collaborating on another film. The Ajanta Cinestone found itself in doldrums and Mr Bhavnani started producing stunt and jungle films of the *Zambo* variety with only an occasional *Awakening*.[2]

Now when, thanks to the comparatively more rational policy of the new Bombay Board of Censors, *The Mill* at last comes to the screen, it has the intriguing attraction of the once forbidden fruit. Everyone who chooses his film fare with a little discrimination wants to see this film because it was once—BANNED!

But Why?

On seeing the picture, therefore, I fail to see why the Bombay Board of Censors took any objection to it. To me, it appeared to be excellent propaganda for benevolent capitalism—and which capitalist ever confessed that he was not benevolent? I think the Millowners' Association may profitably sponsor free shows of this film for their employees. And there is no doubt it will never be allowed for exhibition in U.S.S.R.!

---

[2] *Zambo, The Ape Man* (1937), *Jaagran* (The Awakening, 1936) were films made by Mohan Bhavnani.

There were two distinct phases of the literary career of Munshi Premchand. Always a brilliant writer of Hindustani, most of his life he was a mild reformist—anxious for social reform but not agreeable to too many radical changes. It was only during the last three years of his life that his writings manifested a distinct swing to the left, a progressive appreciation of political and economic phenomena in their true perspective. His election as the president of the Indian Progressive Writers' Association, in the last year of his life, was a well-deserved tribute paid to him by the younger generation of writers.

System, Not Individuals

The Mill obviously belonged to his earlier phase. In this story, he saw the problem of Labour versus Capital as the problem of a few corrupt capitalists who exploited the workers. He did not indict the system but only some persons like Vinodh, the villainous son of Seth Hansraj who inherits the mill jointly with his sister, Padma, who sympathizes (in a patronizing way, of course) with the workers. The Moral appears to be that if only every capitalist had a sister like Padma, there would be an end to all labour troubles—which is quite absurd. Some capitalists do have such sisters, and yet labour unrest continues in their mills! The most benevolent mill-owners cannot 'appease' workers for all times without changing the system.

And yet, *The Mill* is to be welcomed as an attempt to show to the mill-owners how some of them go beyond all limits in their exploitation of workers. It would have served a useful purpose if it helped to soften the heart even of one callous employer. Of course, it deals more with loyalty to the 'Mill' as an institution and gently chides the owners, but has not much to say about the fundamental problems of the 'Mazdoor'.

Within its ideological limitations, Premchand's story yet had ample material for a vigorous sociological drama. Unfortunately, Mr Bhavnani (who wrote the scenario as well as directed the picture) did not make the best use of it. An excruciatingly long death-bed scene gives the film a slow and inauspicious start. Then follow the inevitable chorus songs (sung by working women with plucked eyebrows), the equally inevitable drunken brawls in a dancing girl's house, attempted seductions, the romance of the mill-owner's daughter with an unemployed youth, romantic songs, etc. So that hardly any footage is left for the original theme of the film. And yet, whatever dramatic vigour it has is in the strike scenes—for, after all, conflict (whether romantic or economic) is the strongest foundation of drama. A shot in which a worker is shown clenching his fist in indignation, by itself, has intense drama in it.

It will be unfair to criticize the technique of a film produced five years ago. Judging from average standards then prevalent, it is quite satisfactory.

It is interesting to compare the performances of players in The Mill with their present-day capabilities. Bibbo as Padma was then just beginning to be known for her singing talent. Jairaj looked a promising but raw youngster. Navin (Zambo) Yagnik was still playing minor roles and the comedian Bhudo Advani had but made his debut. Only the veteran Nayampally was then, as now, playing 'heavies'.

For its historical value and as a homage to the late Premchand, The Mill may be seen at the Imperial.

Padosi: The Story of Thakur and Mirza

27 January 1941

This is the story of two neighbours, Thakur and Mirza, and their friendship. A simple story. A true story.

They lived in a little village on the banks of a river. The village was poor, with its mud huts, its uneven streets, its goats and cattle and poultry wandering about in the lanes. It was a village indistinguishable from the thousand other villages in this country, boasting of no architectural landmarks, except a dilapidated old temple and an aged mosque, and enjoying no civic amenities—no electricity, water works, drainage system, theatre, public hall, or parks.

And yet, in the eyes of Thakur and Mirza, there was no place in the world like their village. They loved every brick and every tree of it and every time they saw the cluster of mud huts stretched along the riverbank, their faces beamed with pride, and a strange peace, a sense of security and of belonging filled their hearts.

It was their village, their homes. It had given them birth and they had played in its lap. It was their mother.

Every evening, as the sun went down behind the mango grove, Thakur would look up at the darkening sky and stop his bhajan. For this was the time when his friend and neighbour, Mirza, came out, a rolled-up mat under his arm, to offer his evening namaz.

Their devotions over, Thakur and Mirza would squat on the little bit of ground between their huts and settle down for a game of chess. Great chess-fiends these two neighbours were, and, but for their wives, they would never stop playing. As the shadows lengthened and finally merged into the gloom of dusk, one could still see them, concentrating on each move and countermove like two experienced generals. All the time Thakur's hands automatically played the sarots, cutting betel nuts into little pieces, and Mirza puffed away at his hookah.

The friendship between Thakur and Mirza was shared by their families. Their wives were like sisters to each other, their grown-up sons, Gokul and Naeem, were great pals, and the little children of both the households played together. So deep was the understanding between these two families that if their children quarrelled and had to be punished Thakur would take the side of Mirza's son and Thakur's son would seek the protection of his chacha.

But soon a shadow was cast over the sunny village and the friendship of Thakur and Mirza suffered an eclipse. Men of money appeared on the scene and brought with them an atmosphere of intrigue, suspicion and bitterness. Thakur and Mirza, both men who commanded respect, were obstacles in the way of the capitalists. Under their leadership, the villagers refused to sell their village—their home, their 'tirath', their mother!— for the privilege' of being landless wage-earners. And capitalism, with its calculations of 25% dividend upset, hit back!

Thakur and Mirza's friendship was poisoned by a diabolical intrigue, the seeds of suspicion deliberately sown. The friends of yesterday were no longer friends; soon they would be sworn enemies. Autumn leaves showered where once the flowers of their friendship had blossomed; the cold winds blew across the skies and the neighbours no longer had the glow of love within to keep them warm. Soon they ceased even to be neighbours. The chess pieces lay scattered on the ground—the dry bones of their friendship and their neighbourliness!

But the world cannot exist without harmony, not even the little world in which Mirza and Thakur lived. Their friendship had been the prime motif of the life of each of them; it had also been at once the symbol and the foundation of the unity of the village. Without their friendship to sustain them, both Thakur and Mirza lost their mental moorings. They became proud, irritable, uncompromising, unneighbourly! And the village that once was a happy, united community became the hot-bed of fratricidal strife. Brother raised his hand against brother!

And thus it would have gone on, had not youth—in the shape of Thakur's son, Gokul, and Mirza's son, Naeem—taken matters in their own hands. The desperate situation required a desperate remedy. It needed dynamite and fire; a dam had to be blasted and the pent-up fury of a river released.

And at last, the hands of Thakur and Mirza were once again clasped in an immortal gesture of friendship. They died but they made their village alive again.

This is the story of Thakur and Mirza. This is the story of India, for there are almost 300 million Thakurs and 100 million Mirzas in this country.

This is the story of the Prabhat film *Padosi*, which is one of the very few films produced in any country which has so subtly, yet so successfully, exploited the entertainment value of the screen to rouse a nation's collective consciousness. *Padosi* is at once realistic and idealistic; it depicts social conditions as they are normally and shows that in the natural rhythm and harmony of the Indian village (if it is not disturbed by extraneous factors) we have already got a pattern of social behaviours on which we can base our national unity.

To call it a propaganda film is to insult *Padosi* and its makers, for 'propaganda,' in this age of Goebbels, suggests something vulgar and cheap and blatant. To say that *Padosi* is a picture with a message is equally misleading. Throughout there is not a word of preaching or sermonizing, things are gently, subtly, almost imperceptibly, suggested—mostly pictorially—but never talked about. The allegory is perfect, the symbolisms surprisingly effective. The message, if any, is implicit in the conditions depicted and not in the picture. And yet, like all true art, the picture has an elevating effect on those who see it, like a spiritual tonic that invigorates but does not inebriate.

One of the outstanding artistic qualities of *Padosi* is the perfect balance between its theme and its background. Indeed, so effortlessly does the theme of friendship emerge from the social background of an Indian village that the two are indistinguishable. Indeed one may say that the Indian village itself is the theme—the village with its simple democracy of the 'panchayat' and its camaraderie, the deep-rooted loyalty of its people to the soil, their religious and superstitious nature, uncontaminated by bigotry; their fatalism and their gullibility, the sincere ring of their folk songs and the pageantry of their festivals.

The village, as represented in *Padosi*, is neither idealized as a heaven on earth, as poets and back to the village enthusiasts would like us to believe, nor is it caricatured and ridiculed. Both its strong points and weaknesses are brought out in vivid detail. The old peasant who servilely says, '*Hum to kore kaghaz pur angootha lagane wale hain* (I am the kind who puts thumb prints on blank paper)' is as familiar and real a character as the brave youth who uses dynamite on the dam to save his village. The cringing Jairam is no less an authentic character than the upright Mirza who, when he is elected sarpanch to try his friend's son, forgets everything—friends, relations, children— except consideration of justice.

Many have been the films that sought to depict various aspects of Indian rural life, with varying measure of success. But never before has a village on the screen become so alive, so real, so vivid as in *Padosi*. But for the few romantic interludes where the artist's instinct for beauty and colour, melody and rhythm has temporarily run away with his sense of realism, every single scene bears the stamp of authenticity and sincerity.

To those who have been watching with interest the evolution of director Shantaram as an idealist and a social commentator, *Padosi* completes the trilogy that began with *The Unexpected* (*Duniya Na Mane*).

Aadmi, of course, has yet to be surpassed (in this writer's opinion), even by Shantaram himself, in certain aspects of it—its rugged realism, the daring originality of its camera and sound technique and the memorable characterization of Kesar. But *Padosi* has more direct and vital relevance to the life of the vast mass of our people, and its presentation of a difficult and ticklish theme is unique in its subtlety and restraint.

As for production values and the hundred little cinematographic devices that the director has used to make a social document an absorbing and entertaining picture, Shantaram has once again proved that an intellectual and idealistic approach to film production need not be at the cost of technical qualities. Indeed such an approach must introduce refinements and subtleties in the otherwise prosaic technique. That is why today the most socially conscious film director has consistently given the lead in technical improvements and innovations.

To author Vishram Bidekar, congratulations for a story that will live long in the annals of progressive cinema.

To director Shantaram, not congratulations but thanks for giving us yet another progressive picture and for helping in the evolution of the Indian cinema as art with a purpose.

I hope *Padosi* will be seen from one corner of the country to the other and that in years to come when a grandmother sits down in an evening, with the little ones clustered around her knees, she will tell them the story of Thakur and Mirza, the good friends and neighbours they were and how miserable they felt when foolishly they allowed a third party to sow the seeds of bitterness in their hearts.

Another Hit from Malad Studio

Leela Chitnis Excels in Bombay Talkies' 'Kangan'
2 November 1939

Kangan, Bombay Talkies' latest production at the Roxy, ushers in a new phase in the life of the well-known production unit of Malad.

Planned and equipped five years ago on a scale that was then unprecedented in the history of the Indian film industry, Bombay Talkies quickly established a reputation for superb technique. Working on sound business lines, with a factory-like regularity, their single production unit turned out four or five pictures a year—a few outstanding, some good, none below a certain level and all providing clean and wholesome entertainment.

Franz Osten's Difficulty

One fact, however, was a constant source of annoyance to the well-wishers of Bombay

Talkies: in fourteen consecutive pictures, the same name appeared in the credit titles as director—the name of a foreigner. And while no one doubted or questioned the technical excellence of Herr Franz Osten's work (and those who knew him testified to his painstaking efforts and personal amiability), it was clear that he was unable to infuse into the pictures that characteristically Indian spirit which one finds in the pictures of a [Jahnu] Barua, Debaki Bose, Nitin Bose, or Shantaram. His approach to the Indian social life depicted in his pictures was patently pictorial. The psychological import and social significance of everyday incidents dramatized in his films naturally escaped him. Which, of course, was not his fault. Shantaram, directing German pictures, would be confronted with the same difficulty.

Thanks to the War!

Among other things, the war has introduced vital changes in the personnel of the Bombay Talkies studios. Indeed, *Kangan* was less than half finished when the German technicians, including the director, had to suddenly leave for the detention camp. And the entire film industry breathlessly awaited the consequences. Would the production be abandoned? Would Bombay Talkies import a director from some other studio? Would Himanshu Rai himself direct? Unemployed directors were seen hovering around Malad and certain conceited directors caused it to be known that they were being tempted to go over to complete the picture.

But all these vain 'hopes' and unwarranted fears were set at rest by the completion and release of *Kangan* strictly on schedule! Not a day's delay was caused by the departure of the German technicians and, for all practical purposes, it appeared as if the old director, cameraman and laboratory incharge had never left the studio precincts.

Not only was *Kangan* released on schedule but what at once surprised and gladdened everyone, the technical level of the production has not been let down an inch.

Young Indians' Triumph

The same old excellent standard of photography, sound-recording and processing was maintained. And though it is difficult to judge a picture which has passed through the hands of more than one director, I perceived a certain refreshingly original quality about the handling of certain scenes which were free from the all-too-familiar and rigid Osten touch.

What is the secret of this seemingly miraculous phenomenon?

The secret is that shrewdly enough, producer Himanshu Rai has a batch of educated, highly intelligent young men whom he has kept under training in the various departments of the studio. Quietly and steadily, they seem to have learnt from the veteran German technicians. And on the very first opportunity that they got, they fully vindicated their capabilities.

Of these young men, a few may be mentioned by name.

N.R. Acharya: One of the two associate directors who completed *Kangan* after Osten left. With almost a decade of experience in the industry, he was sometimes one of Debaki Bose's assistants. In the position of production manager and associate film architect, he has played an important part in Bombay Talkies.

S. Najmul Hasan Naqvi (not to be confused with Najmul Hussain, the hero of *Jawani ki Hawa* and *Kapal Kundala*): Also one of the associate directors of *Kangan,* he has been the right hand man of Himanshu Rai and Franz Osten's first assistant. One of the most competent continuity men in India, he also works on the script with Himanshu Rai and collaborates in editing the picture.

R.D. Preenja: This young cameraman who has worked under Josef Wirsching for five years has learnt a lot. Now that he will have independent charge, he is expected to prove himself among India's leading cinematographers.

Mukerji: Hitherto one of the Bombay Talkies' trio of competent sound engineers, he collaborated with Saradindu Banerji in preparing the scenario of *Kangan*, which is based on Gajendra Kumar Mitra's original story in Bengali. He shares the credit for investing the rather 'familiar' story with interesting situations and lively incidents.

Leela Gets a Break

Kangan also marks a new departure for Bombay Talkies in another respect. It is the first film in which they have featured a star already 'made' by other studios. In the few pictures which did not star Devika Rani, they experimented with 'raw' material—Maya, Renuka, and Hansa.

It was a surprise to most of us when it was announced that Leela Chitnis would play the lead in *Kangan*.

The arrangement, however, proved mutually beneficial. For the first time, Bombay Talkies acquired for their picture a really satisfactory substitute for Devaki Rani. On her part, Leela Chitnis got the best role she has had since her sensational debut in *Chhaya*. After that, her talent was wasted and human feeling with which he ultimately unbends to allow his son's marriage give the picture a heart-warming appeal.

Next comes V.H. Desai, who is now more than a mere comedian. There is more restraint and less 'obviousness' in his humour and, therefore, it is all the most entertaining.

All in all, *Kangan* is definitely one of the most likeable films of the year. It is not outstanding. It is simple. It is human. It is entertaining.

in such impossible films as *Gentleman Daku*. In *Sant Tulsida*
had a secondary role—and which young women would r
playing a romantic foil to old man [Vishnupant] Pagni

There can be no doubt, indeed, that *Kangan's* is the f
and completely satisfying characterization she has given
the screen. As the young, unsophisticated adopted dau
of a bajrangi, in love with the son of the local zaminda
is appropriately 'naïve', yet gay and in moments of frustr
she is the very picture of pathos. Her range of expres
is almost unlimited and in this respect she can be com
only to Devaki Rani. One wishes, however, that the rar
her moods and expressions was not sought to be match
such a variety of smart 'saris' which appear incongruous
poor bairagini.

By the way, she reveals unsuspected musical talent a
least two of her songs are memorable for the feeling with
they are sung.

The story of *Kangan* is basically a familiar one: ric
loves poor girl. But it has been enlivened with some goo
original twists and interesting situations. The boy himself
as insipid as Devdas and does take some sort of a stand a
his narrow-minded father for the sake of his love. In thi
Ashok Kumar gets better opportunities than he has got
past. I can't say that he has not improved—he is certain
inelastic—and yet he cannot be said to have reached hist
heights in this picture.

Mubarak and Desai Shine

Next to Leela Chitnis the most remarkable characteriz
is that of Mubarak as the old zamindar. And the solid di

Two Great Kings Resurrected

'Peter The First' and 'Jehangir the Just'
26 August 1939

There is a historical parallel between Peter the First and Jehangir, the Mughal emperor of India.

Peter 'opened a window on Europe' and westernized a feudal, backward Russia. He allowed merchants from western countries to establish trade relations with Russia. Almost a century earlier Jehangir, too, 'opened a window on Europe' as it was in his reign that a British ambassador, Sir Thomas Roe, was for the first time received at the court of an Indian emperor.

Both these emperors 're-live' on the screen—Peter the first in a Russian film of that name at Eros and Jehangir in Minerva's *Pukar* at New Empire, Central and Minerva.

Pukar, which had an unprecedented triple-theatre premiere on Thursday, is a film of which the producers, Minerva Movietone, may well be proud. It is their best effort yet.

To producer-director-actor Sohrab Modi, our congratulations on this achievement. *Pukar* is one of the noteworthy films of the year.

It is remarkable for the painstaking and elaborate preparations that it necessitated, for the lavish expense of money and energy. One can easily believe that it cost over two lakhs and two years to produce.

Taboo Defied

It is specially commendable for it has defied the taboo on Muslim subjects—imposed for some time for the fear of over-sensitive orthodoxy. Kamal Amrohi's carefully worked-out scenario deals with the life of Jehangir and Nur Jehan with respect and understanding, judicious imagination filling the gaps of history with a variety of rich incident.

Depicting as it does an era in Indian history when the Moghals were steadily turning a conquered colony into an 'Indian' empire, giving equal protection and facilities to all communities, and glorifying as it does Jehangir's sense of justice and Sardar Sangramsing's sense of duty, *Pukar* has an ennobling theme.

The picture would have considerably gained in historical—and even contemporary!—interest if the scenarist had interwoven such well-known and epoch-making moments of history as the appearance of the British ambassador at the court of the Great Moghal.

Bells of Justice

But then, *Pukar* only seeks to present one aspect of the life and personality of Jehangir—his scrupulous and speedy dispensation of justice. The bells which clang to inform the king that an appellant was at the door have been cleverly utilized for effect and become the symbols of justice. The picture appropriately opens with them and whatever else happens in the picture they are always in the background, and we have the peculiar satisfaction that one has but to ring these bells and justice will be done.

The film, in its earlier stages, deals more with the feud between two aristocratic Rajput families, the son of one family loving the daughter of the other—the classic Romeo-Juliet affair! The young man happens to kill the father and brother of his sweetheart and then absconds. His father, a loyal officer of the emperor, brings back the errant youth to stand his trial and pay the penalty of law. Justice is done and the young lover is sentenced to death.

Jehangir's problem

Meanwhile, the same pitiless justice is about to crush another life—the queen herself for she, too, has caused the death of a human being. The drama thus resolves itself into a personal problem for Jehangir—duty and justice versus love. Is he to abuse the prerogative of an emperor and let the death of a subject go unpunished? Or is he to sacrifice the one person who is to him the meaning of all things in life? The dramatic way in which this problem is solved is the highlight of the picture.

Chandramohan Scores

Chandramohan, as Jehangir, steals the picture in a convincing manner, even though he does not get as many scenes as the importance of his role demanded. He invests the characterization with a royal dignity and a subtle mellowness and speaks with a crisp intonation that will be the delight of Hindustani-speaking audiences.

Sohrab Modi, who plays the all-important role of Sangramsing, shows an improvement on his earlier performances as he is less stagy now.

Naseem looks the part of Nur Jehan. Sheela scores with a moving portrayal of a sympathetic, subdued role.

The settings in *Pukar* are going to be over-burdened with praise. I know they are impressive. But I am afraid the new looking studio-made 'sets' do not match and harmonize with the exteriors shot in the Moghal forts of Agra and Delhi!

Once again, I have to close the review of an excellent Indian picture with the statement that it would considerably improve by a judicious cutting of the surplus footage.

Who Is a Film Critic?

13 May 1939

Who is a film critic or a film journalist? But then, one might as well ask: who is a journalist? Anyone who has ever written a 'Letter to the Editor' claims to be a journalist and anyone who has seen two films and written a few lines of praise or disparagement parades as a critic. On the other hand, one of the best writers on screen matters in Bombay prefers to hide himself under the modest guise of a 'film correspondent.' Indeed not a few British and American film writers have adopted a designation 'film reporter.' Let us, then, leave it to the readers to judge for themselves.

Not Born

Let's begin by debunking any notion that film critics are born or that criticism is our exclusive estate. Personally speaking, my own chief qualification for writing about films is the fact that

I see, at an average, a film every day and have been doing so for some time. The only essential difference between a critic and a reasonably observant film fan is, as pointed out by an eminent English critic, that the former has 'better opportunities for judging pictures, wider standards of comparison and more practice in summing films up quickly'.

To this I may add that seeing all kinds of films as a routine job and a comparatively closer familiarity with the technical processes of film production tend to give us an objective (you might call it cold-blooded) attitude towards films—so that we are not so easily carried away merely by the glamorous personality of an actress or the glycerine tear-stained climax of a sentimental photoplay, as the average cine-goer is quite liable to do. We also make it our business to study the box-office and on seeing a picture should be able to say, within a reasonable margin, how the public would react to it.

Art and Arithmetic

The ultimate standard of judgement, of course, must depend on the individual taste and temperament of the critic. Art is not arithmetic that the correct solution in every case must turn out to be the same. The films are produced with artistic and technical cunning to appeal to millions. There are all sorts of ways of looking at them—and of writing about them. There are poetically inclined critics to whom the pseudo-mystical atmosphere of Debaki Bose and [Jahnu] Barua pictures makes a special appeal, while there are others who prefer the straightforward approach of Nitin Bose and Shantaram.

One is fastidious about technical perfection, another (like me) may overlook any flaws in photography or sound recording if the film has some originality and its approach to life and its problem is progressive and realistic. Again, trade paper critics must (to be fair to the exhibitors who depend on their opinion to book the pictures) keep in view the box-office appeal more than the other artistic or technical qualities of a film. But in whichever way he looks at it, a film critic should, above all, remain impartial and provide proper guidance to the film-goer.

A Guide

It is not necessary to be mercilessly critical. At the present stage of our film industry, it would be callous to damn the crude (but, in some ways, promising) productions of small studios with a stroke of the pen. But the critic owes it to the producer and to the industry to point out avoidable flaws. And, finally, he to owes it to the fan to describe the pictures correctly to help him (or her) choose an evening's entertainment. There is a demand for all sorts of films—from mythological epics to crime thrillers. It is the duty of the critic to see that he does not send those who would like *Sant Tukaram* to see *Hunterwali* and vice versa! That would be a tragedy and a betrayal of the trust that the public reposes in him.

Culture, Cash and Cinema

14 December 1939

(These are extracts from a paper that was read before the Cultural Conference held under the joint auspices of the Bombay Students Brotherhood and the Muslim Students' Association, and is released for publication through the Film Journalists' Association)

I urge the claim of cinema to be regarded as the greatest, most potent and the most universal art of mankind, and a cultural force destined to produce a revolution in the mind of man, greater than the one that was produced by the invention of the navigator's compass or of the printing press.

Prudery, Snobbery

Not many years ago we had to creep furtively to the picture house when the backs of our elders were turned, as if we were committing a sin. Today more and more people are learning to accept films as a normal feature of our life, like the radio, the aeroplane and the daily newspaper. But I suspect that even among highly educated and enlightened people there is a lurking tendency to look down upon the cinema as an inferior art, not to be compared with painting and sculpture and music. And I am sure that even among intellectuals there will be many who think of film stars only as immoral people and would hesitate to class them among creative artists like painters and musicians. This attitude is universal and is inherited from the prudes and snobs and Mrs Grundies of the last century.

And Inferiority Complex

But in India this attitude assumes an even more vicious aspect, for inferiority complex is added to snobbery. Many of our intellectuals will talk enthusiastically about foreign films and foreign film personalities but betray rank ignorance when discussing Indian films which, they have arbitrarily decided, must be inferior. This attitude can be directly traced to the general ignorance about Indian culture that Lord Macaulay's system of education has created amongst us, so that some people who know Shakespeare by heart have never heard of Premchand and people who can dance the Polka or the Lambeth Walk don't know whether Kathakali is a dance or a disease. Then there are those who, while free from conventional taboos, still persist in the illusion that Hollywood is the vice centre of the world and that films are exclusively meant to provide escapist entertainment.

Facts

Cinema can, or cannot, be a cultural medium developed and used for social ends as a people's art, as long as these fallacies are removed or persist in our minds. It is necessary, therefore, that the thinking people devote some attention to a study of the elementary facts about cinema that determine its course of evolution.

The two peculiar fundamentals of cinema are that it requires a considerable amount of money to make a motion picture and secondly that the co-operation of a large number of persons is essential in this process. All the problems and paradoxes of the film world arise out of these two facts. You can buy a flute for two annas and draw from it immortal melodies. You can take a piece of charcoal and sketch a masterpiece upon the wall. Sculpture is not dependent upon marble; it can be moulded from the potter's clay. The case of the films is quite different.

A Costly Process

Let us take the question of expenditure first. I need not give details but it is easy for you to see why the production of motion pictures is a costly process. Only people with considerable means can afford to produce pictures. And as only an infinitesimal minority of capitalists are altruists, it is clear that the latter must get back their investments—with profit, of course! Only in a socialist society, therefore, can cinema be developed and will flourish on ideal lines. The phenomenal progress, technical and artistic, made by Soviet films is a living proof that the profit motive should be eliminated to allow the free development of cinema, as of all other arts.

On the other hand, we have seen how Hollywood, the film world's capital, continued for years to dope us with standardized escapist melodramas and set up false standards of beauty and human conduct. The capitalist film producers had not only to get their investments back but also in the process to make us crazy about their films and their glamorized film stars so that like drug-addicts we would continue to pay for their dope. In all other countries, the growing film industry inherited this tradition from Hollywood.

No Audience, No Cinema!

But in recent years Hollywood has surprised us by producing an increasing number of films that have definitely transcended the old escapist tradition. Twenty, or even ten, years ago it was inconceivable that commercial studios would send out pictures like *The Life of Louis Pasteur*, *The Life of Emile Zola*, *Juarez*, *Confessions of a Nazi Spy* and *The Good Earth*. How has this amazing transformation come about? It has been made possible by that very box office which is generally supposed to be the bane of cinema. For cinema is a peculiar art, as it depends not only upon the genius of the artist but also upon the patronage of the public. The painter may paint for himself and the musician play in the wilderness, but cinema does not exist without an audience.

Not only commercially, but artistically, the public is an essential factor for the coming into being of a motion picture.

Reels of celluloid lying in tins, even if they contain the finest and most artistic shots, have no value—indeed, they do not deserve to be called a motion picture—unless projected on the screen and seen by an audience. Thus, of all the arts, cinema most directly goes to and is influenced by the general public. That is why I call it people's art. Each person who goes to see a picture shares the credit for its creation—and the joy of creation, too! Thus the growing refinement and maturity of public taste and the increasing interest taken by the people in social, political and economic problems must of necessity be reflected in cinema. That is how Hollywood, while still producing its traditional charming stupidities, is forced, by an indirect and subtle process, to produce some pictures with deeper themes and more significant social implications.

Crude But Serious

In India, which has been experiencing a tremendous cultural upsurge as a direct result of mass awakening in the country and the consequent development of a more serious, critical and socially conscious mind, the realities of life have often been captured even in the shoddiest cinema films. Indeed, I can confidently say that though technically poor, Indian films, in their content, are less escapist than the average Hollywood product. During the past so many years, some of the most popular films have been those which had a bearing on vital social problems.

Learn to Discriminate

This process can be helped and directed into more progressive channels if the thinking classes learn to take more interest in Indian films. Nothing can be more harmful than the present attitude, the two extremes of uncritical appreciation and snobbish contempt.

When you go to a library or a bookshop, how do you choose a volume? By the name of the author, the publishers and in some cases by the press reviews. You have learnt to use this discrimination after years of study and a subconscious process of trial and error. Bring to bear the same careful and serious discrimination in the selection of your evening's entertainments. Study the comparative value and characteristics of the work of various directors. You will find that while Debaki Bose suffers from a surfeit of mysticism and romanticism, Shantaram has a more realistic approach to life; that Nitin Bose gives the best all-round entertainment, and that Jahnu Barua is constantly experimenting with themes as well as technique. You would find that some of the best films like *Badi Didi* prove box-office failures because the class of people that is capable of appreciating them forms a very small minority of film-goers.

Smash The Vicious Circle

And thus you come to the conclusion that the only effective method open to the general public to help in the development of the cinema as a cultural medium is to see worthwhile films. A few idealist producers or directors may produce a few good films. But the Rs. 1-2, 9 annas or 4 annas that you pay at the box office is the ultimate factor for pre-fixing the quality of films. Which again brings us to the conclusion that culture is a legitimate progeny of cash! And so, the vicious circle goes on forming simply another riddle of the universe and of civilisation. But this should all the more spur the builders of the new civilization towards recognizing the growing MENACE, if not IMPORTANCE of cinema as a potent generative force. If the atom can be smashed why not this vicious circle?

The Screen as a Teacher of Hindustani

Indian Talkies are Helping to Evolve a National Language · 19 January 1941

It is fashionable in puritan nationalist circles to run down cinema as an immoral institution. Sometimes it has been classed with wine-drinking and 'satta' gambling! Even the highbrow 'moderns' assume an attitude of superior indifference and are often heard to remark that Indian cinema is only an escapist form of cheap entertainment, fit only for those with the crudest taste and wholly devoid of any cultural value. This is not the place to discuss at length all the pros and cons of Indian cinema as a cultural force but it may be worthwhile to mention at least one aspect of it. Cinema, in my opinion, is the greatest teacher of Hindustani that we have and it has done more than any person or institution to propagate and to popularize the national language. If we are really serious about developing Hindustani as the language of the Indian people, it will be most unwise to disregard the great service that the screen can render and is already rendering to this national cause.

Purely Accidental Beginnings

Let me hasten to remove the impression that the screen came to be instrumental in spreading the national language by a conscious effort of the producers. With a few exceptions, these gentlemen, like true capitalists, are innocent of any patriotic motives nor can they be accused of possessing a constructive imagination. If their films have helped the spread of Hindustani, it has been purely accidental—or, at least, subsidiary to their main material considerations. Perhaps they themselves will be most surprised to hear of any relation between their films and the evolution of the national language.

The propagation of Hindustani through the screen began with the advent of the talkies in India and was determined by purely economic factors. Long before the present Hindustani movement took shape—before, indeed, the very term Hindustani was adopted as the proper name for the national language—Indian film producers were faced with a linguistic problem. The problem interested them because it affected their pockets. In the days of the silent films it was possible to show the same pictures all over the country. Their 'language' of action was universally understood. With the introduction of the spoken word in the films that universality was gone and the film market was restricted to the area where the particular language used in the dialogues was understood. The early Indian talking films were of two types—romantic versified melodramas like *Layla Majnun* and *Shirin Farhad* adapted from the stage, in which the

language used was high-flown Persianized Urdu, and the
religious dramas based on Hindu mythology, in which the
language used was equally high-flown Sanskritized Hindi.
Soon, however, it was found that to make the former popular
among the Tamilians of South India was as difficult as to
make the Muslim population of North India rave about the
latter. The commercial instinct of the producers pointed
towards a compromise between the two linguistic extremes,
thus making the dialogues in their pictures understood by
the largest number of cine-goers all over the country. The
result was the evolution of the Hindustani of the talkies—a
not very elegant or literary language, a curious mixture of
Hindi words like 'prem' and Urdu words like 'manzil,' but a
language that had a chance of being understood in Calcutta
and Bombay as well as in Allahabad and Lahore and even, to
some extent, in Mysore and Rangoon.

Problems of Lingua Franca

It sounds presumptuous but I do believe that long before the
publication of Common Language Readers and even before
the term 'Hindustani' gained currency, the Indian talkies
were helping to evolve a common national language. Without
hair-spitting literary discussions, without importing racial and
communal prejudices into the controversy, they had solved
a practical problem in a practical manner. When our literary
experts sit down to compile the first official Hindustani
dictionary, I will suggest to them to see half a dozen popular
Indian films and in their dialogues, they will discover at least
a rough draft of their dictionary. I would be the last person
to advocate the adoption, wholesale, of screen Hindustani by

the lexicographers of the national language. It can be used only as a basis for further investigation. By trial and error, through their efforts to make themselves understood by the cine-goers in the remotest corners of the country, from Tuticorin to Peshawar, by their literary tight-rope walking to avoid the pitfall of difficult Urdu on the one hand and difficult Hindi on the other, the humble dialogue-writers of the Indian films have taken the first practical step towards the final evolution of Hindustani. It will be only profitable and practical to take advantage of their experience.

The contribution of the Indian screen to the evolution of Hindustani as the national language is two-fold. Not only has it helped, as already indicated, to assimilate a large number of simple, commonly understood words into a new vocabulary but, what is even more important, it has familiarized millions of people in the non-Hindustani-speaking areas with this vocabulary. Ten years ago, it was rare to find a South Indian able to understand and speak even the simplest phrase in Hindustani. It was practically impossible for a visitor from Delhi to make himself understood in Bangalore, Hyderabad (Sind) or Chittagong. Today the situation has vastly changed and thanks to the inroads of Hindustani films in non-Hindustani-speaking provinces, it is possible for a Punjabi and a Tamilian to meet on the streets of Nagpur and to converse with each other.

Influence of Hindustani Daily Increasing

Tens of thousands of people whose mother tongue is Tamil, Telugu, Kannada, Sindhi, Punjabi or Bengali, are daily thronging their local cinemas showing Hindustani films and, lured by the glamour of Kanan Bala, the melody of Saigal and the histrionic ability of Devika Rani, they are being drawn into the ranks of the votaries of Hindustani. The influence of the Hindustani films can be gauged from the fact that the films in provincial languages have totally failed to challenge their supremacy and today a Hindustani film makes far more money in South India than a Tamil or a Telugu film!

Here, then, are at least ten million cinema fans who have acquired a rudimentary knowledge of Hindustani from the screen. While seeking only to entertain them, the films have taught them their national language. For any plan to spread and develop Hindustani, this vast number ought to be used as a nucleus and the widespread instinct to be entertained should be pressed into service of the cause of the national language.

How can this be achieved? It should be the task of Hindustani scholars to find that out, in consultation and in cooperation with literary men in the film industry. I would like leading dialogue-writers for the screen to be invited to work on any committees that may be set up to evolve a scheme for the propagation of Hindustani in all its various aspects. Not only should they be requested to lend the benefit of their experience for the purpose of preparing a Hindustani dictionary but, in their turn, they should be asked to popularize the use of correct yet simple Hindustani through the dialogues in their pictures. Prizes could be offered for the year's best dialogues in a film, works of fiction in Hindustani could be recommended for filming and generally an increasing contact established between the film world and the literary world. Then it could be pointed out that the life of Tulsidas, the first great Hindustani poet, should not have been produced in Marathi! Indeed, the considerable resources and influence of the persons and organizations engaged in the work of evolving and spreading the national language could be used very effectively to encourage the production of films in Hindustani only, aiming at a gradual elimination of the films in the provincial languages. And, finally, why not a film or a series of films dramatizing the very theme of Hindustani—tracing its evolution since the days of Tulsidas, through the Moghul period when the impact of the two cultures produced a new common language, the era of Kabir and the early 'Brij Bhasha' poets, down to the present age? Here is the ready-made scenario of a really national picture—a with plenty of action (It was in military camps of the Moghuls that the language originated)—fine dialogues, exquisite songs (written by the greatest poets of many centuries from Tulsidas to Kabir and Ghalib), entertaining humorous interludes (Imagine a Tamilian trying to barter his Tamil with the Pushto of a man from the frontier and both realizing the necessity of a common language!) and even romantic moments (Wasn't Akbar's marriage with Jodhabai a step in the direction of the evolution of Hindustani?). Does it all sound comically fantastic? Perhaps. But if produced with imagination and the proper historical perspective, it can be turned into a really fine and purposeful film, an unparalleled historical saga of the screen. And let us produce it if only to deal with the final blow to the short-sighted snobbery that refuses to acknowledge the screen's cultural potentialities. The films have already taught Hindustani to ten millions. Why not use them also to spread the national language to the remaining 340 millions?

From 'Harishchandra' to 'Adhikar'

Quarter Century of Indian Films[3]
6 May 1939

When Indian cinema-goers saw on the silver screen, for the first time, the presentation of a familiar story in an indigenous atmosphere and acted by people like themselves, no wonder the producers were amply rewarded for their enterprise and the picture was successfully shown all over the country. A few production units later sprung up at Calcutta and Madras and the pioneering producers were kept busy coping with the increasing demand for Indian films. There were, of course, no studios worth the name, most of the shooting being done in bungalow compounds, and it was not until 1920 that artificial lighting was used. The actors were largely borrowed from the stage while only singing girls were available to act the feminine

---

[3] 1913–1938, Indian Motion Pictures, Jubilee Supplement, *Bombay Chronicle*.

roles. The stage technique, indeed, permeated the whole process of film production and the Indian stage itself was at that time in a degenerate stage, providing cheap entertainment to the mass of illiterate people by producing crude versified plays. Painted scenery curtains were used instead of 'sets', the gestures and action of the artists had the theatrical touch of crudity and unrealism and even the costumes were of the same hybrid tawdry variety that were affected by the players in theatrical productions. Equally strong was the influence of the stage in the selection of themes and stories. Mythological plays were turned into mythological films and the lore and legends of ancient India were gone through in search of filmable material.

Italian Actress in Indian Film!

Following the success of Mr Dadasaheb Phalke's venture, more and more financiers were induced to invest their capital in this business which, even in those days of post-war boom, could yield better and quicker profits. By 1919, Madan Theatres of Calcutta had started production of films. Originally, they were owners of cinema houses and producers of conventional stage plays and this experience proved to be a distinct advantage to them. Their very first picture, a 'mythological', was a great success. It is interesting to note that the leading feminine role in this film was played by an Italian actress. With the conservative communities still regarding film work with suspicion, it was difficult until very recently to secure the services of intelligent and presentable educated young women. The Madans hit upon the idea of employing Anglo-Indian girls, many of whom proved successful and popular stars.

End of Mythological Era

The year 1920 may be put down in marking the end of
what may be termed the exclusively 'mythological era' of
the Indian screen. By now hardly any episode from the
'Ramayana' or 'Mahabharata' was left which had not been
filmed and indeed, some of the more popular legends had
been produced over and over again. While today, when there
is a cry for sophisticated and modern pictures, one is liable
to regard mythological films with disfavour, one cannot
deny that they did serve a useful purpose by establishing the
screen as a popular medium of entertainment, thus laying the
foundation for the latter-day progress and prosperity of the
Indian film industry. The vast mass of conservative Indians
would not have taken to the innovation of the cinema had they
not been drawn to it by their age-old interest in mythological
lore. There is a limit, however, to the stock of story material
in mythology and when a number of new producing concerns
came into being in 1919 and 1920, they were faced with a
shortage of potential scenarios. They wanted something
different from their age-old interest in mythology. Thus
started a cycle of Rajput pictures, which sought to win public
favour with spicy tales of martial heroism and chivalry with
the stunts and thrills of Wild West films. Rajput history and
legends were ransacked for suitable material and when even
this was exhausted, resourceful producers started adapting
American adventure films into Indian atmosphere and
so was born the pure stunt film. To appeal to the popular
imagination, such films were packed full with the most
amazing exploits and adventures, impossible acts of heroism
and superhuman feats of athletics. This was the time when

the 'hero' fought an army of men single-handed, brandished a tin sword and arrived always on a galloping horse just in time to save the heroine from the clutches of evil-looking fellows, ready to do the He-Man stuff. Successively popular were several variations of the stunt films, Douglas Fairbanks' *The Thief of Bagdad* starting a series of similar action pictures in India. The next important step was the detective thriller which, for the first time, brought the modern atmosphere on the screen. Among these will be recalled *Kala Nag*, *Telephone Girl* and *The Wild Cat of Bombay*, the last-named being the film which made Sulochana famous and incidentally gave birth to the star system in India. These were known as 'social' films, to distinguish them from the historical and the mythological films. It is difficult now to trace the origin of this term but in the parlance of the Indian film industry, 'social' is still used to describe a film in which the atmosphere, settings and costumes are modern.

While the evolution of the 'social' film was taking place, the cine technique, too, was making steady progress in India. Better and more cinema houses were built and there was a general demand for films of a superior quality. While it was no doubt true that producers were motivated by the desire for quick returns and minimum investments, there was a distinct improvement noticeable in the equipment of the studios as well as their products.

'Light of Asia'

The year 1925 will remain an important landmark in the history of the Indian cinema, as it was in that year that an Indian film was released in the international market. *The Light*

of Asia, based on the life of Gautama Buddha, was produced by
the Great Eastern Film Corporation of Lahore in collaboration
with a German concern, the Emelka Film Co. The film was
tremendous success in England and on the continent and
was followed by *Loves of a Moghul Prince*, based on the historical
romance of Emperor Jehangir and Anarkali. Both these films
were of a high technical standard and to a great extent, it helped
to raise the general level of cinema technique in India.

In Bengal

Meanwhile, film production was making a headway in Bengal
too. Several new studios were started and some of them made
a bold attempt to give something new to the film-goers who
were by now fairly sick with the profusion of mythological and
stunt pictures. Themes touching upon the real social problems
of Bengal came to be in demand and, though their appeal was
limited to the province, they served a most useful purpose by
introducing vital and realistic stories and using cinema in the
cause of social reform.

The production of some stories of Dr Rabindranath
Tagore further helped to raise the cultural level of the cinema
in Bengal film production found a fertile field in this province as
it had already established traditions of dramatic art. Very soon,
educated Bengalis started taking to this line, efficient technicians
were trained and the Bengali stage contributed a large quota of
competent film artists. Hence forth the leadership of the film
industry definitely passed from Bombay to Calcutta.

Along with the speedy development of the Indian film
industry, which was within financial limitations, modelled
on the lines of Hollywood, methods of publicity and 'star-

manufacture' came to be employed by producers and names
like Sulochana, Gohar, Patience Cooper, Zubeida, Vithal,
Bilimoria brothers and Jal Merchant became known to screen
audiences all over the country.

The Talkies Arrive

Such was the state of affairs when the era of the talkies started
in India. After a few experimental 'shorts' had been made, the
first full-length Hindustani talkie, *Alam Ara*—a romantic costume
film—was released by the Imperial Film Co. of Bombay. As a
sheer novelty the picture proved to be a great hit and soon every
other studio in the country had to go in for talkies. The Madans of
Calcutta were the next to exploit this field and produced a number
of popular musicals. They were still staging plays and thus they
found it easy to use the same materials in talkies. Other producers,
too, combed the theatrical companies for artists who could act
and sing. Thus it was that the earliest Indian talkies inherited
the high-flown language, the versified dialogue, the exaggerated
gestures and the profusion of songs from the decadent Indian
stage. All popular stage hits were quickly turned into talkies and
the Madans reaped a rich harvest from films like *Laila Majnu* and
Shirin Farhad. At one time it almost seemed as if the Indian film
had got stuck in the mire of cheap musicals and would never be
able to reach heights of real artistic and technical achievement.
But actually the talkies proved the salvation of the Indian cinema.
The increased cost of production killed all mushroom studios
which could not afford to go in for the expensive equipment
necessary for talkie-production. At the same time, the big profits
made by the earliest talkie hits induced bigger financiers to lend
their support to the film industry. Larger and better-quipped

studios came into being and distinct technical improvement
was noticeable. During the silent days, the actors and actresses
were engaged for their looks and athletic skills, respectively,
irrespective of histrionic ability. With the advent of the talkies
many of them had to go and there was a demand for educated
and cultured artists. The cinema theatres increased, the crowds at
the booking office swelled and the Indian film industry was now
finally set upon the path of prosperity and progress.

Prabhat and New Theatres

Since the advent of the talkies the pace of progress has been
quickened, thanks to the efforts and achievements of an
increasing number of progressive producers, some of whom
may be briefly mentioned here.

Prabhat Film Co. of Poona, founded nine years ago at
Kolhapur by a band of enthusiastic technicians working on
a cooperative basis, was the first well-organised attempt to
produce pictures of quality. Even its earliest mythological
films were marked with excellent technique and authentic
atmosphere. Elaborate 'sets', spectacular scenes and
impressive mass effects have been the special features of
Prabhat productions. Until recently they specialized in
'costume' films but their first 'social', *The Unexpected*, too,
has achieved outstanding success. To them belongs to the
credit for producing *Sant Tukaram*, a film of extraordinary
artistic excellence depicting the life of a popular saint, which
established a world record by continuously running for
over two years and won a prize at the International Film
Exhibition of Venice.

About the same time as Prabhat was founded New Theatres in Calcutta. Drawing upon the cultural resources of renascent Bengal and at the same time collecting an efficient and cosmopolitan staff from all over India, this studio has quickly gained a position of eminence with its series of good productions. New Theatres were the first to interest eminent writers like the late Sarat Chandra Chatterji and Pandit Sudershan in film production, to raise the level of film music and to generally give their films that touch of refinement and technical elegance which had been lacking in Indian films. They have today the largest number of established stars and the best directors and their films are noted for artistic elegance.

Bombay Talkies

The first Indian studio started on sound business lines as a limited liability concern is Bombay Talkies. Ltd. With the assistance of some of the leading financiers and staffed with expert Indian and foreign technicians—some of whom had been responsible for *Karma*, the first Indian talkie to be produced in England—it could afford to set up the most perfectly equipped studio in India and, within three years, Bombay Talkies pictures have already achieved an enviable reputation. Perfect technique is the outstanding feature of their productions and it is not wrong to say that in this respect they have helped to raise the general technical level of the Indian screen. Their excellent film of Harijan life, *Achhut Kannya*, was among the best Indian films produced in recent years.

Among the other companies, Sagar Movietone have recently come into prominence by producing stories by such well-known Gujarati writers as Mr. K.M. Munshi and with their smart and sophisticated comedies like *Three Hundred Days and After*. Huns Pictures of Kolhapur, though handicapped by limited resources, are gaining a reputation for progressive and enterprising productions.

There are many other studios employing about 35,000 workers and producing 350 pictures a year. Some of them, it must be admitted, are still engaged in the production of 'popular' stunt pictures, cheap comedies and crude mythologicals. But these are definitely on the decline even though now and then some of them may produce a picture which is a box-office success. Even the much maligned 'popular' taste shows a definite change for the better and a comparative study of the recent box-office hits would reveal that quality pictures are steadily ousting the 'quickies' from the market.

What of the future? While none need be pessimistic about it, keen students of Indian cinema are agreed that in the ultimate analysis further progress will be conditioned by the expansion of the present limited market available for the Indian films. There are only about a thousand cinema theatres in the whole of India while a country like Great Britain with a much smaller population has about five thousand! Moreover, while the British and the American productions have a world-wide market, Indian talkies have perforce to depend only on these thousand cinema houses. The profit on a film thus does not warrant expensive production and most of the producers naturally cannot afford to buy better stories, engage better artists and technicians and to use the superior studio equipment necessary for really first class productions. Pending a substantial increase in the number of cinemas in the country, it might be profitable to explore the foreign market—especially the countries and colonies with a substantial Indian population. But only the best Indian pictures have a chance of being popular abroad and it is advisable that there should be coordination between the efforts that are being made in this connection by some of the leading producers. But even a world-wide market will be gained by us when producers change their present production policy and plan their work on more intelligent and rational lines.

When Death Stalks the Studios!

Unfortunate Accidents and Their Lesson: Will Motion Picture
Congress Consider the Question of Compensation?
5 April 1939

An actor, Mohamed Rafique, died the other day while a scene
for a film was being 'shot' in Sagar Studios. It appears that he
failed to jump out of the way of a car that was to smash through
a gate and received fatal injuries.

We mourn his death with the deceased's family.

Every such happening reported from the studios raises the
all-important issue of insurance of studio employees against
accidents as also the question of compensation to be paid to
the dependants of the victim.

They must know their Rights

I believe there are one or two studios that have insured their
workers against accidents. What about the rest? Is proper

free medical treatment given to workers who may be injured while working in the studios? Is there some provision for compensation to be paid to the wounded, the disfigured and the disabled? The studio workers must know, and exercise their rights under the Workman's Compensation Act and if in some respects, their cash is not covered by existing legislation, there must be an agitation for a special enactment.

It is possible that the producer feels reluctant to pay adequate compensation as the whole amount must be paid out of his pocket. In that case it is in his interests as well as his duty to insure his workers against accidents.

Avoid Risks

In film production, particularly when 'stunt' scenes have to be 'shot', there is an attendant risk. But with adequate and intelligent precautions, the risk can be minimized. Goodwill is not enough, the producer must also strive to evolve methods by which film production, as far as possible, becomes proof against accidents. A really capable director must, by circumspection and technical subtlety, avoid all risks. In Hollywood it is being done. Even crashing aeroplanes on roof-tops has been rendered practically safe. And proportionate to the vast extent of the film industry in America, there are much fewer accidents in Hollywood than in India.

Legion of the Lost

Leaving aside minor injuries, etc. which are seldom reported to the press, it has been a pathetic record for last year.

A technician died of electric shock owing to leakage in the cables through which high voltage current must pass for powerful studio lights. Did his dependents get any compensation?

Another studio worker died when a cracker burst in his hands during production.

Three actors were drowned in the Pawai lake where a scene was being shot for a film. And again one wonders if their families were paid any compensation?

And now Mohamed Rafique has joined the legion of the lost. His death is a poignant reminder of the need for immediate action.

Will the forthcoming Motion Picture Congress, in the midst of their discussion about duties and tariffs and dividends and percentages, care to devote some attention to the question of compensation for studio accidents?